Martin Seymour-Smith

Collected Poems
1943-1993

Edited and introduced by
Peter Davies

GREENWICH EXCHANGE
LONDON

Greenwich Exchange, London

First published in Great Britain in 2006
All rights reserved

Martin Seymour-Smith
Collected Poems 1943-1993
© Estate of Martin Seymour-Smith 2006

Printed and bound by Q3 Digital/Litho, Loughborough
Tel: 01509 213456
Typesetting and layout by Albion Associates, London
Tel: 020 8852 4646
Cover design by December Publications, Belfast
Tel: 028 90286559

Cover photograph courtesy of Seymour-Smith family

Greenwich Exchange Website: www.greenex.co.uk

ISBN 1-871551-47-1

Contents

Introduction   vii

POEMS 1943-52   1
  He Came to Visit Me   3
  The Sacrifice   3
  Green Wall My Grave   4
  Child after a Storm   5
  Flight of a Dove   6
  Imagined Child   7
  Week-End   8
  Despair   9
  Men of the Island   10
  Winter for William   12
  Entrance to Hell   13
  A Mother in Sunlight   14
  She Is Afraid of Dawn   15
  New Year   16
  Cursed Harlequin   16
  Lancelot   17
  Don Juan in Hell   18
  Beauty and the Beast   19
  Voyage to an Island   20

POEMS 1952   21
  Fortunemaster   23
  The Infant Man   25
  Questions on the Staircase   26
  The Shape of Love   27
  The Dead Lover   28

ALL DEVILS FADING 1953   29
  Elegy   31
  Furies   32

A trial in Dream   32
Birds in his Head   33
All Devils Fading   33
No One Will Know   34
The Pool   35

TEA WITH MISS STOCKPORT 1963   37
The Lights on the Water   39
The Victims   39
The Punishment   40
Forthcoming Attractions   41
What Schoolmasters Say   42
The Change   43
The Northern Monster   44
The Rosy Captain   46
To Passers-By   49
Blitzenkrieger   50
The Last Chance   54
The Execution   57
Found on a Building Site   59
The Administrators   60
Living by the River   62
Request on the Field   63
Poor Fatso   64
History Lesson   65
Tea with Miss Stockport   66

REMINISCENCES OF NORMA 1971   69
To Sally Chilver   70

SATIRES
The Invitation   71
Queen Leer   73
Censor Jack   73
Sunday Morning Walk   74
I Have Never Felt   75
The Cruel Gravy   76
To All Watchers over Public Morality   77
A Versifier in Private   78

THREE IMITATIONS

    Fredrico Garcia Lorca: 1910 (interval)   79
    Umberto Saba: Winter noon   80
    Fernando Pessoa: Poets   81

    Reminiscences of Norma   82

OTHER POEMS

    Mistral   92
    The Blue Trumpeter   93
    Pathétique   95
    The Answer   95
    Saxelby   96
    In the Market-Place   97
    Pinchbeck   98
    An Observation for Unverifiable
        Reconsideration in a Game Perhaps   99
    The Cellar   100
    Why   103
    To Miss Parfitt (1934) Sadly:
        This Poem about Dying   104
    Girl's Song   105
    The Words   106
    Speech from a Play   107
    Questions before Parting   108
    In Memoriam – Brian Higgins 1930-1965   109
    Beach, 1737   110
    Tuthill's Enormities   111
    In the Hotel   113
    The Shore   114

WILDERNESS 1994   115

    Wilderness   117
    The Lonely Ghost   118
    North   119
    Obstacles   119
    Influenzal   120
    I was a Young Man Once   121
    Unsmiling   122

To My Wife in Hospital   123
A Scrap of Moonlight   124
Chrysanthemums   125
Colloquies   126
The Word Machine   127
Nothing   128
Different Imaginations   129
The Messenger   130
In My Eye   131
Rachmaninov   133
Silverhill   134
Après un Rêve   135
Being Invented You   136
Pool of Light   136
The Love Toucan   136
The Shawl   137
Your Look   138
Appetite of Quiet Enchantment   139
Mars in Scorpio   140
There was Never   141
Forgive us, Women   142
After Tagore   142
A Sort of Love   143
The Internal Saboteur   144
Reflections   145
Eyebright   146
Letters   147
She to Him   148
To My Daughters   149

Index of first lines   151

Index of titles   155

Introduction

ALIENATION is perhaps too strong – and since Brecht, too loaded – a term to describe the poetic art of Martin Seymour-Smith. Yet undoubtedly he gave the impression of being a figure inhabiting the verges of society, and frequently looking in on it with perplexity. That is not to suggest that there was anything bloodless or marginalized about the man or his work. For Seymour-Smith, man and writer, personal relationships were the very stuff of life. A passionate engagement with them is the meat of his finest poetry. In it, sexuality is an inescapable fact of being.

Society in the mass, even literary society, was something with which he had a less easy relationship. Though he loved to talk – and did so long and fascinatingly, often on subjects which might well have nothing to do with literature – he was not at his best in the salon, and never formed a part of any côterie. It was perhaps this that led to his being undervalued, even ignored, as a poet while he lived, and judged almost entirely on his work as a literary biographer, reviewer, critic and editor. In whatever he undertook in these fields, be it his superbly annotated old-spelling edition of Shakespeare's *Sonnets* or the highly accessible popular compendium, *Novels and Novelists*, his scholarship was consummate and his judgements compelling.

To the general reader Martin Seymour-Smith was best known for his 'big' literary biographies: of his friend Robert Graves, of Rudyard Kipling and of Thomas Hardy. These were scholarly, readable and, in the case of the last two at any rate, apparently 'controversial', though Seymour-Smith himself (perhaps not entirely ingenuously) could never quite understand why. There was, to the end, a good deal of the imp in him.

Then there was his outstanding *Guide to Modern World Literature*, which was first published by Wolfe in 1973 and was reissued – revised and greatly expanded – as the *Macmillan Guide to Modern World Literature* in 1986. On its first appearance the *Guide* was greeted with a mixture of puzzlement, disbelief and, in some instances, sheer jealousy by reviewers. That such a magisterial survey could be the work of one man in an era when works of its type are commonly assembled by teams of contributors, invited scepticism in some quarters, while it compelled admiration in others. In fact the book, which, in its second edition ran to some three-quarters of a million words, gained immensely from the unity of purpose and the blaze of passion for literature that lay behind it.

What was not fully understood by the sceptics was the fact that the *Guide's* author was fundamentally a creative writer, and was well acquainted with the precariousness of that condition. He knew, in the words of Keats "that there is not a fiercer hell than the failure in a great object". He wrote of poets and novelists and playwrights not merely as a critic, but with the compassionate love of a fellow maker who has, with them, striven to do well and yet, at the end of a long night, known what it is to stare failure in the face.

Poetry was his primary calling. It was not a pursuit for the mental interstices between the writing commissions he had to undertake to support his independence – though the toll those exacted on his time was undoubtedly responsible for the smallness of the output he chose to see published. Notwithstanding the scale of his œuvre in the critical and biographical fields it was primarily as a poet that he was regarded by Robert Graves, Norman Cameron, James Reeves, C.H. Sisson, Robert Nye and Philip Larkin, who included him in his *Oxford Book of 20th Century Verse.*

Seymour-Smith's kinship is with poets of the 17th century. He shares their love of argument, ratiocination, and, above all, a constant wrestling with the self. He has been compared with Henry Vaughan, though he lacks Vaughan's mystical temper – and his freedom from guilt. In the wryest of his love poems he is capable, rather, of recalling Donne or Marvell, though he himself admitted to the influence of a poet from a very different era – Browning. Certainly he shares with Browning that gift for sinewy, colloquial discourse which makes us almost always want to take the poems off the page and share their insights, out loud, with others. In his early verse Seymour-Smith is undoubtedly, in terms of style, in some thrall to Graves and Cameron. But these influences are soon sloughed off, as a highly individual voice and sensibility develops, at once passionate, sceptical – of himself and his motives, as well as those of others – eclectic in its tastes and replete with irony.

Martin Seymour-Smith was born in Stoke Newington, London, on 24th April 1928, the only son of the librarian and bibliographer Frank Seymour Smith. His mother, Marjorie (née Harris) published verse as Elena Fearn. Seymour-Smith was educated at Highgate School from where, in 1946, he was called up into the Army. After completing basic training in England he spent most of the next two years serving as a sergeant in Egypt.

In the Army he boxed with great success at bantamweight and a certain pugnacity, physically and in argument, never left him. But it was not a Hemingway-esque pugnacity. Indeed, he wrote amusingly in the *Guide* of Hemingway's pretensions to martial accomplishments, and could not abide his simplistic attitude to women.

After being demobbed Seymour-Smith went up to St Edmund Hall, Oxford, where he read history and was poetry editor of *Isis*. He had known Robert Graves since, aged 14 and impelled by his admiration for a poem he had read, he had packed an attaché case and travelled to Devon to seek the poet out. The two men became friends and on graduating in 1951 Seymour-Smith accepted an invitation to go out to Majorca as tutor to one of Graves's sons.

At Oxford he had met Janet de Glanville, who was reading Greats at Somerville. She went with him to Majorca, where they were married in 1952. She helped Graves with much of the raw material for his *The Greek Myths*. Though her mind was thereafter at intervals to fall prey to its own brilliance in episodes of huge depression, it was always at the service of Seymour-Smith's prodigious critical endeavours, and he frequently submitted his judgement to the bar of hers. In all vicissitudes it was a partnership in which the life of the intellect was shared.

Returning to England in 1954, Seymour-Smith taught in various schools for the next six years, liking the children but, character-istically, not much relishing either the disciplinary or bureaucratic side of the school regime. In 1960 he went freelance, supporting himself and his family thereafter by reviewing poetry for most of the major newspapers and periodicals at one time or another, and through commissions for books. These were not solely literary, but included such sociological studies as *Fallen Women* (1962) and *Sex and Society* (1975). In 1958 he had moved to Bexhill-on-Sea in Sussex, where his two daughters grew up and where he was to live and work until his sudden death at the age of 70 on 10th July 1998. Janet died two months later on 2nd September aged 68. It was a passing, as Robert Nye observed in his obituary notice in *The Independent*, that was "more a matter of completeness" than of the pneumonia that was diagnosed.

Periodicals and anthologies apart, the first appearance by which Martin Seymour-Smith can be judged in the round was his sharing, with Terence Hards and Rex Taylor, a volume *Poems*, which appeared from Longmans (Dorchester) in 1952. In Seymour-Smith's case the selection ranged back to 1943. The opening poem, 'He Came to Visit Me', is the utterance of youth, yet it boldly announces its metaphysical intentions:

> He came to visit me my mortal messenger.
> I saw the sorrow stamped upon his face.
> He bade me chide at him for grief. 'But sir'
> I said, 'you know your dominating place.'

Stylistic influences notwithstanding, this is poetry of precocious self assurance. Its challenging last stanza sets the poet off on a course which is increasingly to diverge from that of the Movement poets – anthologised by Robert Conquest in *New Lines* (1956) – and their programme of steadfast reason and moderation:

> So death it was he knew behind that sheet
> Of skin; darkness behind its passive light. And all
> around him, while he spoke, there beat
> The endless drummers of subtracting night.

Setting out his stall as a love poet, too, in this collection, Seymour-Smith sketches what is to be a theme explored with increasing complexity as his output unravels: the capacity of sexual love to inflict psychological damage on those who dare it. This, from 'The Sacrifice':

> She wounded him and bound his wound,
>   Laid her cheek against his face,
>   And felt his heart alive with love.
> She hurt his wound and when he groaned
>   She kissed away his pain, and thus
>   He felt the fate within him heave.

is characteristic in its concerns.

There were further appearances — essentially as a pamphlet poet — in No 10 of the *Fantasy Poets* series (1952) issued by the Oxford University Poetry Society, and with *All Devils Fading* from Robert Creeley's Divers Press, published in Majorca in 1953. In these, the inner life and the sexual relationship are explored with ever deepening intensity. Stylistic influences have by now been shrugged off in verse which is becoming freer, but nevertheless retains a high degree of adherence to form.

In the title poem of *All Devils Fading* the poet ruefully, but also with a sense of glimpsed horrors, tries to come to terms with that insistent antagonism-in-affection, and sometimes downright cruelty, that are so often at the heart of the erotic life:

> 'You were never divine,'
> She says, 'and over your affairs
> The shadows will always incline,
>   Closing it in, it is your anger
> At nature,' she says, and stares.
>
> Why then, with her slight smile,
>   All Devils fading, does she give
> Me her hand and close her eyes,
>   Thus, in her sorrow to beguile
> My Death? It must be she too dies,
>   But with no love to forgive
> Me for her own betrayal.

At this stage Seymour-Smith's reputation was still very largely among cognoscenti. *Tea With Miss Stockport* (1963), which included some of his previously published poems, brought him wider attention.

The volume continues, with ever-increasing vividness, and sometimes disillusionment, the examination of the sexual relationship which was to preoccupy Seymour-Smith to the end of his life. But many of its poems explore another, darker theme: an increased sense of alienation from institutional mechanisms, and the threat to the individual imagination posed by the procedures of bureaucracy. The protagonist of these poems is often seen as being no more than washed-up flotsam on life's foreshore, a man at best unvalued in his own milieu, at worst cast out and sunk into total dereliction.

Thus, the bleak lines from 'Found on a Building Site':

> I am naked on a building site
> In Penge West. It is 1.5 am, and cold;
> The mist wreathes round me, rising in columns.
> I shall have much to think of, but chiefly
> What shall I do at dawn?

come over not as an exercise in bohemian cant, but as the quiet despair of a mind that has, somehow, found itself become completely beyond the social pale.

In 'The Execution' the protagonist, now formally condemned to death, finds a form of salvation in the refusal of the sceptical lions, to whom he is thrown, to accept their proffered prey from the hands of the authorities.

This theme is elaborated in the title poem, 'Tea With Miss Stockport'. Its apparently good humoured anarchy (the protagonist alone of her weekly visitors has the wisdom not to patronise the old lady, and escapes the grisly fate she has in store for them) is in fact in tune with the collection's sombre theme – namely that there are few bolt holes in the modern universe for a sensibility that is fundamentally at odds with the conformist spirits who predominate in it. In her fundamental scepticism, and in her recognition of decency Miss Stockport – like the lions – represents at least one such focus of eccentric, but vital, honesty.

The exploration of the man-woman relationship reaches its most intense in *Reminiscences of Norma* which appeared in 1971. At the core of the volume, which also contains satire, imitations, wry observations on growing up, friendship and growing old, is the series of 'Norma' poems which give it its title. In them, the poet evokes with naked honesty the powerlessness of (in this case) the man who is in thrall to sexual love – and that condition's mysterious capacity to confront the individual with his/her own total loss of self respect:

> It is well for you tonight pretty girl
> To put on your dancing stockings and twirl twirl
> In exquisite clubs of drink and lust
> While I rack myself with jealous thoughts
> Of brute sailors smirking
> And your crushed self finding in their tattoed arms
> More sweetness than in my foolish love.

The ambiguity of the sexual situation, with its hoping-against-hope quality, is savoured in the poem's final stanza:

> Yet how can I believe
> That when you take down your hair
> And come to me smiling
> Your heart is not there?

In the penultimate poem of the series the poet imagines himself the spectral undertaker of their love, its ashes symbolised by Norma's body, stiff, cold and never again to respond to his – or any other's – caresses.

> I left you Norma and you died alone
> In that room whose ancient places stopped the sun.
> Then from the street towards you there crept one
> To wash your body lying on our dark bed:
> To sponge your thighs still filthy with my sperm
> And kiss pale lips that once were red and firm.

More than 20 years separate *Norma* from Seymour-Smith's last published volume, *Wilderness: 36 Poems 1972-93* (1994). The distillation of a large output over that period, which included much in the way of experiment that he chose not to publish, a certain amount flung over the shoulder in spurts of irritation, and a considerable amount of translation, much of which comes into its own in the *Guide, Wilderness* displays in its apparently small compass, an astonishing range of tone and concerns. The verse has become simpler and more pliant. The voice is that of an older man – but in no sense that of T.S. Eliot's "aged eagle". True, there is something more than mere ruefulness in:

> I was a young man once
> Never was one such;
> I lived
> In a water-wheel
> And heard no music
> But my own.

though the regret, if such it be, is always tempered by the strong irony lying at the core of the poet's being. Seymour-Smith's ability to make an apparently commonplace phraseology go to work as the vehicle for poetic utterance is seen in such a poem as 'Chrysanthemums':

> Everybody's chrysanthemums,
> Everybody's,
> Are a good dream that will come true.
> And you know as I know
> From their sombre colours
> Staunch against the heart-withering,
> Calamitous, mind-shrinking, encumbering,
> Deadening, torturing
> Bleakness of weather,
> That all dreams enable,
> Enable,
> Love to break through.
> Look now at the trees,
> Stripped as if dead,
> At the unbreakable ground:
> Look with your battered mind's
> Too consequential sadness.
> Do not miss
> Those red, russets, profound dark yellows:
> Late, late,
> But hardy,
> Perennial.

This enlisting of the activity of the natural world as the tangible parallel of man's condition *sub specie aeternitatis* is a quality Seymour-Smith shares with his admired Thomas Hardy.

When Seymour-Smith first contemplated a successor collection to *Reminiscences of Norma* in the 1980s he gave it the working title 'The Internal Saboteur' (a term used by the psychoanalyst W.R.D. Fairbairn). That poem does appear in *Wilderness*. It concludes with an impassioned litany that might stand, appropriately, as the coda for a creative life that never at any point rested on its laurels, but continued the 'mental fight' to the finish:

> Give me the grace at last to understand
> The language of God's creatures at their end.
> There's such divinity within their lack
> As would give me my conversation back.

Peter Davies 2005

POEMS 1943-52

HE CAME TO VISIT ME

He came to visit me, my mortal messenger;
    I saw the sorrow stamped upon his face.
He bade me chide at him, for grief. 'But sir'
    I said, 'you know your dominating place.'

'That's it,' he said to me, 'you spin the thread
    Of life in me; you make me flesh and blood,
Although we both wish now that I were dead.
    This sorrow on my face is but a hood;

Behind there is a blank white wall of skin —
    An eyeless, mouthless, noseless face: neutrality.
It is dark death that lives behind the thin
    Pale flesh. You have my eyes, I cannot see.'

So death it was he knew behind that sheet
    Of skin; darkness behind its passive light.
And all around him, while he spoke, there beat
    The endless drummers of subtracting night.

THE SACRIFICE

    She wounded him and bound his wound,
    Laid her cheek against his face,
    And felt his heart alive with love.
    She hurt his wound and when he groaned
    She kissed away his pain, and thus
    He felt the fate within him heave.

    She knew that he would surely die;
    His wound stung with her tears.
    She called the fire within her heart
    Brightly to burn at her red lips;
    She kissed him, weeping at her loss:
    And only left the heart, the fate.

GREEN WALL MY GRAVE

This green wall to which I turn for sleep
    Has told my curse upon its shining face.
In it, true-reflected, I have seen
    The land that is my dwelling-place.

'O grave, O grave, when will you let me sleep?'
    All night I asked; the wall became the sea —
My drowned past selves came up, each one alone,
    And with the quarter-striking bells, mocked me.

The firelight flickered on the wall,
    Showed me the houses I had known and lost:
But I was dead, and as I watched
    The bugle sounded my last post.

But in this death at last I knew
    The living of a perfect grief and once again
I held my weeping love, and from her tears
    I now return, in this thin rain

To my green wall. The fire is out,
    The bells are cold as still they sound
The quarters to a light I wait not for
    In a dark which I have not found.

Then comes the dawn: the early trumpet
    Blows the dead fire ashes far away,
And as I sleepless grieving rise
    I realise that to-day

We storm our enemies the flowers:
    I strike them down to make my woman weep,
And with her crying still I cry
    'O grave, O grave, when will you let me sleep?'

CHILD AFTER A STORM

I know that before a storm my hands
    Are murder: they follow time
  And make a pattern of my hate
  Across the flowers, create
    The gathering clouds which are my crime.
It is their fury, which your heart defends,
  Makes this wind rise up and desecrate.

The storm hangs low about The Towers
    And you cling frightened to me then:
  So all my fears of death are gone
  As if the sun had never shone
    For we had made our story in that sun,
Have seen our future in these hours –
  Our phantom child of storm alone:

We will not wake him, he is sleeping now.
    I see stretched across the flowers
  Spiders' webs that do not move;
  And the sun shines down upon the roof
    Of the storm-beaten tall wet Towers.
But do not wake him: such storms show
  His sleep across our years will be enough.

FLIGHT OF A DOVE

This morning over the town
There flew a dove.
Its watchers saw
Innocent deviation
In its purely fatal flight;
But I, alone in my room,
As it plunged down,
Then upwards flew
Felt my heart break,
Marked in myself
Such perfect death
As only that dove knew.

IMAGINED CHILD

Her other lover in a hated city
  I knew, and she beloved.
What dreams were there to call upon?
What pity to plead for when only
Her passive face hung on my wall?
  So in my rage at her, I moved
That mask, forbore to call
Down future lanes, my son

Who was a far-imagined child
  That I had conjured
In imperfect hope. But there was none
That sleepless night: so, mad and wild
I broke with cries my deepest vow
  But found my loving was not cured.
'Possible seas, O drown me now!'
I cried, but heard my son

In murmuring sleep, her tears, both real:
  And thus I loved her more
Who for her child, and mine, could weep
Although I knew she came to steal
Him from my mind, although I knew
  Her useless beauty from before,
Yet loving her, what could I do
But turn – as my child might in sleep?

WEEK-END

A week-end at last in his splendid castle,
The Lord of Love's. If, Pandar-like
He walks the balconies, and all of gold,
It is because he does not understand
Each lover's lustless kiss, like ours,
Of which we can (we said so firmly then)
        Be justly proud.

Such honour to eat at last with gusto,
But at pure tables: elude with joy,
And right, that pandar-doubt. Why! he does not
Know the meaning of his own flowers here
That through the gold bars wind and hang,
Pure signatures of love. He (we said)
        Never knew love.

But Monday morning is back to work,
Entered figures and cold tea.
At the mid-week meeting forgotten
That honoured invitation. Indeed,
It is to swear with faces
Turned away in shame that we will never
        Go there again.

DESPAIR

I found her hovering, beautiful
    On the edge of my despair,
Which all evening hung like the light
    Shining above her there.
She was a bird, unwilling
    As that instant, and my eyes
Yearned to her implacable horizon,
    Towards which, with bird-like cries,
She flew. O were I daring morning
    To light her way to the sea,
Yet, dark against my embracing sky
    She'd fly away from me!

MEN OF THE ISLAND

This side of love, the island is
Dependent for its future
On the cry of birds, or tree-whisper;
Depths in sea or mind are stirred
By children diving, or their tears.

Our lives were not intense,
But we lived satisfied, loving
The women here and the land,
And keeping sure in our hearts
The ways of sun and rain.
But there, on that dark coast
Which faces this, gaunt-cheeked
They carry guns to shoot
What evidence there is to show
Love moves them with its laws;
They organise their fears,
Severely re-enact the joy
They might have found when guilty,
Young, incompetent.

Trembling here upon the shore,
In pleasure still, we must
Remember that this sea is theirs,
And theirs the boats that cross;
Our food, for love or life,
Is loaded by their natural ways.
Forget, in spite, we might have said,
Swim off to private rocks.
But this was not enough
Soon we must cross, and fall
On the mainland's different roads,
Victims of our true content.

O with what fear that day
We faced the sea where often
We had played in joy: as children,

Or as boisterous wooers of those
Who wept at our departure
Knowing our return would be
As sea-crossed carrion-birds
Who would settle on the sand
Where once we stood, and caw.

We in their satiated cry confess
As dead we cross the sea
That we were ruled by other loves
Than those which gave us joy.
We feared the coast, knew it was death,
Yet could not resist the journey there
Thus to return, dark birds,
To haunt with fatal knowledge
The rocks where innocent we'd climbed
And fill this island with despair.

WINTER FOR WILLIAM

Winter for William, who lives far off
In a sun-bound island of calm skies,
Will be fairer and finer than for us:
Declined as heated roofs defy
The descended frost. But his eyes will fill
When leaving these cold-growing shores
The ship hoots out her last farewells;
And birds, too, he will see,
Fast flying from threat of snow.
Horizons create such tears
In a child's eyes: he feels the wind,
And tugging at the sleeve cries
'Leaving this island, no no!'
Sorrowful its harbours will not open
To steady the rock and motion of his heart.
But ship and birds move away,
And England becomes farther,
Which he feels as colder, in rocks and in rain,
Through the hiss of the sea-spray, and mist.
The sea is wild, outgoing.

We, who are exiles at home,
Remembering his toys and play
In warmer and greener gardens than now,
Will wonder at our memory of sun
For the sake of one who is not cold.
We will wander in some sleep earlier
Than was ours before, in these bitter seasons
Of deep and ageing snow; spend winters
As warm as William's are.

ENTRANCE TO HELL

In that cloud of grief at our private farewell
The rescuing angels failed to descend;
Instead, we were tapped on our shoulders
By brusque devils: 'This is the end.'
And both were led to separate prisons
To wonder how could the other betray
So purposely? And in hate to dwell.

But in those cells through endless day,
Lonely at last, we make love by knocks
On the wall: to discover sympathy
In separateness, and combine in mind
Against the loveless enemy.

A MOTHER IN SUNLIGHT

Crowding her hours
Of light falling among familiar trees
Are sorrows as whole-yearly
As the autumn afternoon is chill —
But her griefs are personal:
The exact brownness of leaf
Haunting her wide gaze.
This a homage of her four-seasoned mind
To the hours' demands,
Time's local twinges at the heart.

Recipient of such sorrows,
Each day's colour and echo,
Her straining absent son
In the cold autumn weather
Feels himself blessed, redeemed,
Although he is distant, yet
Loving at home the shape
And movement of shadows,
Light's autumn habits there,
He might be below her window,
Still an innocent child
Playing in other autumns
Through her impersonal sleep.

SHE IS AFRAID OF DAWN

She is afraid of dawn, a sin in hope
Haunting the window where the light
Comes slowly through. For he upstairs,
Her husband, dearer in mind than love,
Makes clear that he, till death, is all.

At the edge of each same day
She rises against the cold, to light
The lamps, make fire and tea,
Not looking at the window,
For light is her only love, whom
She must not, till he surrounds her, see.

Lifting her head from the lamp,
Hearing the stove hiss, she sees
In the door a man: not his face,
But the lines of travel, and hard bone.

She cannot compromise, but must recoil,
Having known for so long this visitor
Would come. Softly, slowly,
She turns her head away,
Watching easily at last
The window; he is in the dark,

Amazed that he must move away,
Smelling lamp and stove,
And seeing with love the simple stuff
Of her dress. She is left
The mortal centre of his grieving dawn.

Gone across the lightening fields
He wishes to become the day,
To caress her spurning gentle face;
But turns into the sun: east
Is direction of his journey back.

But she moves singing: knows now
The half-light, a face at last
Unbewildering and familiar.

NEW YEAR

Then turn your head. It is easy
For the music is behind the wall;
And behind your eyes a vision
Of kisses as the slow notes fall.

As time is cruel, marks joy as dreams,
Consumes their promise as singing
Swells, falls and fades in air, so now
You sense such strange awakening

In foreign arms, and yet your own.
They call it futureless, yet how you weep:
Your heart so full of hope to dare
Histories of similar sleep.

CURSED HARLEQUIN

O harlequin, you know too late
What loss too-closeness always makes,
Its curse increases in each nearer kiss.
It is an unseen and a clear,
A rescuing, transparent glass
Delivers her from you and you from her.
But your straining fingers touch
The glass that keeps you separate:
Now where presses her dark hair
A mirror is, in which you stare
And see desire too much.
And with what wondering
You find the blood, the graze
Across your hand! But she is gone,
And in the mirror is a shattered face
Not yours before: yet her tears will fall upon
That ghost, she is still pitying
Your rage to reach her there.

LANCELOT

Lancelot's last and only love was merely
A fold of sleep not dream-explored,
   A mountain in virtue unascended.
His brow's deep lines were never scored
By a lover's heart too unattended,
   But battle-gained, securely.

Desolate seemed his shield: worriedly he eyed
That emblem which in idle kissing
   He had never watched, and yet at which, when true
In love, he needless stared, thus missing
Her heart's moments wild and few.
   And at such lack of him, she cried.

When he turned back to her, she wept again,
Rejecting him in visions of
   His future blood and death. And guilt destroyed
The hero then: her true love
Became distraction; she still toyed
   With that shield so feared by men.

He went away to die; and she to sleep returning
And her futurity, made prayer
   That his doomed heart should fall in pain
And forfeit reason to despair.
Exhausted by desire, she wept again:
   What's done is done when vows are burning.

But still he could not fall, and kept his post
Without the shield: so murderously
   He thrust. Each death was fresh
To show he was himself the enemy:
But could not fall: no old ease of flesh
   Could equal that defeat. He is love's ghost.

DON JUAN IN HELL

Handsomest of all men now beyond the range,
The girls' delight, a former starer
In mirrors, to catch an angle of face, strange
Or familiar, which in their eyes made him fairer;
The gorgon got him at last, in shape
New to his heart, a foreign beauty. And wisdom fell
As the wind from the peak: his wish to escape
Ignominious, he being condemned to ignorant hell.

Half-heartedly he gives up every dream and ghost,
Each mirror hour and casual kiss;
His five children and cold wife are smiling hosts
In those four walls once his; he is unhappy now to miss
The sight of steamers near the coast,
The touring girls; but still notes he is free
In thought or private speech: his one night out he boasts
Of how he used to cheat and take them all
Until her voice from home rings out, calling that key
To all feminine disaster, wrack, and fall.

BEAUTY AND THE BEAST

Stand on this shore and watch – the sea
Corrodes it, as the years her heart.
    But only the beast who loved her knew
The ships on which she might depart,
How much she yearned to be free,
    How the colours in her life were few;
    But her desire for change still grew.

She asked at last, so many sailing:
'Why must this beast haunt my sight
    Wreathing my days with his flowers?
Because at my door he sleeps at night
I have pitied his failing –
    It is like mine, therefore his powers
    Can never change the sneering hours.'

'But my heart is a villain,' she said,
'How can he change if no love is?
    Then I will love him evermore.'
And in this love she gave her kiss:
Then, rising with a handsome head
    He took her to every foreign shore
    But she cried: 'O where is my home
             and my beast of before?'

VOYAGE TO AN ISLAND

Watch what the sun can do, because you died
In my arms, upon this shore: further
Than words' meanings from a land my own —
There you cannot fall into my bad dreams
So perfectly enacted in the mainland city
Whose swinging harbour-light
Sweeps the hill, and lights our way out
On a journey to a different shore.

Watch what the sun can do: I could die
In your arms now, knowing that further along
The mainland shore than you can hear
The wind warns: 'Beware of too much truth,
Beware of the island: watch what the sun can do,
Though there you do not fear its burnings
It will force you to mirrors to mourn
Your killing mask, and kill you too.'

But now I see that three-flowered lamp
Which only in the dark your beauty swings:
It sweeps your face, the hill, the harbour-shore —
How can I ever fear the sun again?
Watch what the dark can do: I will live
In your arms in the brightest valleys
For your private stare lights everything
And I can wake to say: 'Admit the sun.'

POEMS 1952

FORTUNEMASTER

A fortunemaster, whom the sun selected
As all heroes' aggregate, denied the promise,
And made a grave of every aspiration
For Love's sake, because it was this
Defeated the magnificent peregrination
Which he loathed, but history expected.

'What do our mouths yearn to express?'
He asked. 'The sun's but wounded, only slowed
The clock;' then heard his own voice tell
Ambition was the clock whose hands showed
That in true love there is no parallel
Of time and timelessness.

Faith not forgotten, nor yet a toy,
He looked down upon that grave
Of hopes, saw guarding it, the expert in
Departures that no love can save
Or ease – one whom he loved, his bull-head twin,
The enemy he would one day destroy.

'Was it not Love herself enchanted me
Into this mystery of days, but for whose sake?'
He spoke thus against the cities and the fame
That everywhere he could not help but make.
In its burning, he forgot the name
Of the sun that blessed him on the sea.

But he sought respite from seas' alarms:
His cities already old, and his cheeks lined
With the long departure: and grieving
Always for beauty he could not find
He lay with Queens or whores, now not believing
They were thunderbolts held in his arms.

Where Love lived, were tears on his map,
It was from her lands came
The prophecy of how his twin would die.
'O wisdom' he prayed, 'the related bird
That flies above me, guiding, in the sky,
Let me not kill, but from myself escape.'

He saw the white bird's cradle-flight,
And knowing its cry as hers, knew victory
Was certain then — it was that dismay
Which struck the bull-twin down: he could see
The circling bird above him all the day
Of that heroic and unwilling fight.

Chastened, in his loss he sought to bless
The grave and foolish, with such love filled
That they on hills the climb forget: Love
Lived longer than his heart was whole, and killed
The wounded sun: thus was the dying of
Such history-making bitterness.

Unwounded and applauded, yet he falls:
Love has moved him in his conquests
More than the sun pretended.
Tender his eyes for white birds' nests
And for all her signs. But as she intended
At what wrong times his half-heart calls!

THE INFANT MAN

An ill wind blowing, the fearful man
Takes from it the worst he can,
His infant name; and as that boy
Will be the ill wind while it blows.
Your face is strange, curved to destroy
The child while he most nobly grows
In struggle to be your sunlight king.
But you have not done anything.

All night your bed he lay upon –
Destroyer, what could you have done?
My heart you had to fail to break:
Its infant half you took by storm.
This you remembered for my sake,
And like a mother kept him warm,
Made quiet the wind – but thus he died
As the price of being identified.

The memory you do not hate
Of one so helplessly inanimate –
As normal objects of your day
Which love-denying, you bring near.
No more there is my heart can say
But how you stole away its fear:
What mysteries would cease to rack
If it knew the richness of its lack.

QUESTIONS ON THE STAIRCASE

How will you destroy me, love?
 Tonight you stop me on the stair
 With ghost-signal of despair.
 Why do I hesitate? O where
Could I cast off the habit, love?

Is he your messenger of loss
 Who in the mirror by my side
 Stands silently? Are you his bride?
 Am I moon cursed to be denied.
And live within this mirror, loss?

How will you love a ghost
 Against whose cold you had complained?
 When I to comfort you remained
 Had you already entertained
Familiarly that ghost?

Thus imprisoned and alone
 His actions I must imitate
 Although he watches me in hate;
 I am a ghost, and dumb to state
My killing features are his own.

THE SHAPE OF LOVE

He sought to define the shape of her love:
Horizon's clear-cut lines ended
Her landscapes he had explored –
His gaze forever limned them;
But the sage outlines of her will
Deluded his mere following eyes
Until certainty distressed them
With suspicion: 'Whose woman is she?'

'Follow behind me, then! speechless,
While I trace those never altering heights,
Stand on that very skyline
With yourself alone, that none other
Shall with me view its beauty.'

But he could not know the contours
When walking there: and she speechless.
Pride said: 'You will not ask.'
And he called: 'Back to your own land!
I will find this shape alone
For in your other lover's hand
Whom I will kill, the map lies.'

Tinged with blood of many heroes
And proud lovers, his lance denied
All promises: dripped red
On every face or map of hope
Until he had been the whole earth over
And returned to her land, lost.

She slept, and he saw the sun set
On familiar hills, warming his cold heart –
'What have I destroyed, love, what?'
But she, waking, was speechless;
Dark swallowed the hills
While her eyes said: forever now
We must in virtue lie apart.

THE DEAD LOVER

Bells for a death rang early
Through the mist wreathing
Your discontented garden:
The trees and flowers
He had tended, blessed, denied.

Is he not dead —
No longer agile centre of
Your need to find a demon dear
Whose end would end
All garden blossoming?

Yet he it is who died,
And your fruit is not denied.
His grave reminds
There could be other days
Of more withering unrest
And you are blessed
By what your sorrow finds:
No ghost dies
But loving also stays.

ALL DEVILS FADING 1953

ELEGY

It was a stranger child, she knows, than I
    Who loved her first. Not I, but I, he stepped
    From a dream where while she slept
He, kissing lips he thought death-white, lay by:
And thinking her a fantasy, took rest
    In caressing her cold arms. Waking,
    He fled from this dream, her breath breaking
That safe love he nursed in his breast.

I saw her wheeling by a dusk-lit lake
    A child not hers, in ordinary afternoon:
    She was an elegy for some departure, soon
To tear anatomies of love, and make
Each loathed child her own. The sunlight
    Hovered for an instant on the haunted water:
    To leave that child her dark familiar daughter
Who cries out mischief and all ruin in the night.

So moving away from all past sorrow,
    Care, or joy, I follow her from today to today
    In no dream, forgetting my fear of her way
Which leads to real and undreamed death tomorrow.

31

FURIES

They were servants of a beauty
    From whose dangers I had run.
For her they dogged me, to forewarn
    Of stricter times to come.

Too pettily she drove them on,
    And so our friendship grew:
I showed how venal was the act
    Which they were prologue to.

They sing this story now for fee
    And when in streets I hear their song
I go to seek them out: poor souls
    To cast a coin among.

A TRIAL IN DREAM

Dreamer, there are no synonyms
For that white dress you grasped
So beautifully in sleep.
                The church whisperer,
Slanderer, aisle-lounger,
Dozing into incense fantasy
Saw you lean to her
Reaching;
        in such double dream
She was not fallen then.

And yet he spoke, hounding the evil
From us, making the town clean.

BIRDS IN HIS HEAD

Her violent birds in his head he wished
And to find that secret at full moon went
To a swamp's centre, where sweating
He stood in his boat and howled
'Take me at last, for your mystery's sake!'

And her answer thus: hundreds drowned
That moment in a distant sea
(Innocent they leapt from the shelving decks)
Now his pain only their wingbeats
In his head. And guilt at all such deaths.

ALL DEVILS FADING

All her devils here tonight,
    Duly expected: a sour mouth,
And ache in the head, and her voice
Ceaseless in anger. In blurred sight
Angels on her wall rejoice
    At a sudden end of drouth;
But here, still this blight.

There were no easy years:
    Always, in glut, a vague hunger
At spring. 'You were never divine,'
She says, 'and over your affairs
The shadows will always incline,
    Closing in. It is your anger
At nature,' she says, and stares.

Why then, with her slight smile,
    All devils fading, does she give
Me her hand? and close her eyes,
Thus, in her sorrow to beguile
My death. It must be she too dies,
    But with no love to forgive
Me for her own betrayal.

NO ONE WILL KNOW

No one will know these houses are the same
As once they were, controlled in sprawling ease;
    Only for me they changed,
    Have lost the nearness now
Which fills my mind with her to tease
    The guardian scarecrow
    With what she said to me:
'There's no life in a scarecrow's eyes,
No one but me need know your lies.
    No one will know.'

No one will know she is a ghost adored,
That when she said to me 'Goodbye'
    All whisper of this record
Was destroyed: the houses on the hill
Became commonplace as yesterday.
    No one will know.

O ghost of a love in my heart, you came
    A deathlessness to show:
The landscape changed, and with my sight
I read the truth of your surprise.
    Where is that landscape now
To tell this story of betrayal?
    I am the scarecrow.
    No one will know.

THE POOL

Love is a dead image, treeless pool changing
With only the weather.
By your side, I dream
You speak over the still depth
In winter's sullenness
Words you have not spoken
Of exile
And grief moves the water...

Its leafless banks in summer
Are a refuge place
Where present desires
By the past are weathered
To seem like love...

In different seasons' light
I circle it; or in hopeful sleep
Move idly my hand
In the not-changing deep;
Watch the movement I make
Become still as I wake.

TEA WITH MISS STOCKPORT 1963

THE LIGHTS ON THE WATER

The drowned know the sea is wounded
In fame only, when those lights slash
Across the stillness of the port:
Within its honoured depths they taste
The salt of after-action's quiet.

THE VICTIMS

The bells ring signal of judgement at last,
Of immediate burning. We are among
The milling crowd to see this sentence passed,
And hear each whisper: 'What has he done wrong?'

Why are we here at all, who know the best?
Is it because we also have no wealth?
Because, like him, we have no purpose left?
(Who stands at all, stands where he stood himself.)

It is our own bells, swinging, will not spare
Our tender hearts. The congregation
Looks at God on the steeple, supreme up there,
Pointing them home after long conflagration.

But we are crushed by them, elbowed and spurned,
Who know each is the priest, the burner, and the burned.

THE PUNISHMENT

Of all men living, who could be most wise
Insists that women may put out men's eyes;
Yet is himself protected from this ban
On love without obedience: he can
Inform the world that he's contented now
In a serene potency, and broadcast how
He lives happy in a woman's grip –
Ignorant he holds the hand that holds the whip,
Whose punishments therefore produce
Routine reports, no more, in Love's Official News.

Has cold theory caught this rebel up at last?
Are his days of fruitfulness all past
Now he guides her by whom he says he's led?
Or, though he's not yet blinded, sacrificed or dead,
May not she, in fact, have sprung the last surprise,
Already used her cruelty – not his to subsidise –
To cut him, just a little, down to size,
By simply closing up, not putting out, his eyes?

Yet he's so restless on his tranquil rack
How harsh are we who wish such torments back
As would once more his whole frame wrench and crack?

FORTHCOMING ATTRACTIONS

How few are not possessed by private joy
When guns appear like magic in the hero's hands;
And mourn the bristly villain's duty to destroy
The nobler killer of the bright bad lands
Who, better groomed, his evil better understands.

Is this a wish to have correct careening?
Or does ashamed excitement really hide
A subtler facet of the story's meaning?
Do you not find yourself identified
More with the wicked than the righteous side?

The Macbeth type, who has an evil seed,
Avoids the sadness of life-sentence, or the rope
(His social end both censor and your pleasure need)
By dying in self-sacrifice on some sheer slope
Abandoning his natural but wrong-minded hope

He thrusts himself in front of child and wife,
Falls, victim to a gun that never missed.
Like you when plunging into normal life
Drilled full of holes by your psychiatrist,
Your unfired gun clenched threatening in your fist.

And he who killed you without caring,
That simpler villain, truth, dies drunk and swearing.
But will come back next week, and yet more daring.

WHAT SCHOOLMASTERS SAY

What schoolmasters say is not always wrong.
'You're a good chap, Smiggers, but don't go to seed'
Said Pettitt in bathtime at school long ago.
He seemed so earnest that I nearly cried;
But up until now I've laughed at his warning
Of where disregard of his words might lead –
Until last night when I dreamed I had died
   And Pettitt was God.

Hank made us lay out our beds like soldiers;
After Cert. 'A' he summoned me, scowling
'Vile boy, I see that you've mucked it again!'
Of course, I didn't care then: I was proud
And resigned from the Corps against his advice –
But heard Hank's voice with its military sting
As today I strode through the playground crowd:
   'Well, Smith, you've failed!'

I pity myself that now I'm a puppet
Like Hank, and Pettitt, and roaring Gubbo;
That I must answer, when asked by my friends
'If you take your pupils aside and say:
"Vile boys, this won't do, disobedience is wrong,
And if you don't know it I'll make you know!"
Do you *really* mean that those boys should obey?'
   'I may, in a way.'

They are singing this morning before me
'How wonderful' etc. 'must thy sight be'
And if their croaking cannot quite mean God
Nor can it quite mean me. I ask myself: what
Should it mean? Their heads incline, I bow
My own, until a colleague warns: 'Hey, old
Boy! Head up, and watch for talking: *we're* not
   Expected to pray!'

THE CHANGE

I held you close O warm you lay
  Where dank familiar peeling walls
Proclaimed an end of warmth and day.
   'Here, love, no gleam of daylight calls,'
I said. You answered with a sigh:
   'I am afraid of such nightfalls.
    O do not let me die!'

'But die,' I said, 'for death is night,
  We are alone, these walls are steep,
You cannot climb from here to light,
  Therefore give me your fear to keep.'
You did not love but you spoke gently,
  So near you were to me and sleep:
   'Comfort me and I'll die!'

My pleading now turns to despair:
  The basement walls grow thin, recede
Till we inhabit empty air.
  How shall I follow where you lead?
For you have wings, I cannot fly,
  I drop to earth but for your need:
   O do not let me die!

THE NORTHERN MONSTER

At my utmost North of endeavour,
Beyond experience or prayer (landscape
But in imagination's failure
Proved) a bloodless emblem of my hope

Shuffled alone to the enfabled Pole
That bland monster of post-history
Which love itself, with pity's uncontrol,
Invents, to give the sensible cold eye

Promise of familiar heavens,
Convincing the heart wasted by desire
In apt intricate and mortal visions
Of the final wisdom of its fire.

Then, loved one, learning that all I longed for
Was real in you, I renounced hope and struck
Its sign from thought. I murdered metaphor.
I burned that beast and watched its smoke go up,

Love's ideology destroyed, your warmth
Its end. And I resolved therefore that you
Should occupy the impossible North,
Yourself its secret Pole to guide me to.

Oh, but compassion's gift is merciless,
Lover: delusion's ghost cannot forgive
That in its element, of my distress,
I cruelly make you, you unkindly, live.

Dumb ignorance which before had been
Prayer's effigy, as shrieking fire returned,
A corpse that would not be consumed, whose scream
Tormented me with how my purpose burned.

I had forgotten, in a mortal heat,
The distance of love's act from its intention:
That boundless North, which threatens to defeat
Both love's reality, and its invention,

To which I sent you home! The howling grave
Is innocent again, by your love calmed,
Made native there. But how like a beast I rage
To be your Northern monster now, transformed!

THE ROSY CAPTAIN

The mind destroys the scene before it sees:
Half-roses haunt their images that please,
And love itself, before it flowers, divides
Into an icon — and a fear which hides
In nightmares' fantasies, safe flights of prayer,
Catastrophes that threaten everywhere —
Hope's epicentre, whose focus is despair.

But all such phantoms loll drugged in the head
If he shams dead:
That captain whose deathless sleep preserves
The picture-roses mind's half-world deserves.

Beware of concentration's appetite:
The true rose challenges hedonic sight,
Its terror-half steals colour from delight —
The captain who was flesh, though pale and still,
Is now a doll, rose-cheeked. Roses can kill.

Eyes look inwards, then. In asylums' glare
See all that they'd shut out and could not bear;
They hunt a gleam of pity to reflect
Into the wrecked rage-dazzled intellect
But there's no pity there:
War's instruments rule all. The fingers itch
To speak, the mouth is drawn. But which is which?
What once was clear in view is killed by mind:
Escaping eyes turned outwards cannot find
Colour or brightness while freed phantoms sing
That true roses are the dangerous thing.

Scarred vanity must cancel waking quests
For beauty, as absurd; the captain's death
See as maturity's strange sign of age:
As we grow older we forget our rage
And plan more coldly to destroy, record
Half-truths whose chaos we have seen and heard
Too casually in memory; we make

Them into pretty views, appreciate
The clearer enmity of hostile day
Until love challenges the long delay
Of its whole rose, refuses the pretence
Of prayer's or dreaming's half-experience:
Its concentration's demons now demand
One rose, and seek the captain secretly.
Circumstance becomes an enemy
Whose hidden face is only never kind
Whether confronting, so un-care-lined,
The narrowed stare in its contorted frame
(Ghost waked by trouble to proscription's fame)
Or as disaster's dream, whose time and place
We torment into treason's single face.

Remember that pretty picture-postcard view
We'd tucked away? The road we never knew
To a white precipice; the squat homely
Hut of a coastguard who must be friendly
But was not there? Such unheeded pictures
Become histories of betrayal:
No one was near those cliffs who did not fall;
Assumption's weatherbeaten features
Reveal themselves as rosy-smooth, to teach us
How dishonour names the secrets that we live by —
Delusions in which madmen drown and die.

A face cast off as nightmare long ago
Could not inhabit landscape so
Innocently stored in mind, we say:
There is no terror-mask in ruin's day!

But wherever in death-giving rage we went
Was in bewilderment;
Could love itself be trusted to condone
What only unremembered dreams have known?
We walk down that simple road, go in
The hut, but find no coastguard there: instead

The rosy captain, with a doll's bright head,
Sits wooden there. So accusation's dead:
Obscured at last its stare? Destruction's bare,
Bereft of mind's phantoms? Are we safe here?

But as we watch, the eyes are opening:
The waxed cheeks crease and break; and menacing
A finger's raised... We try to plead we meant
Peace only, or that anger's innocent —
But feel ourselves by puppet's wood weighed down
And paralysed our lidless gaze is shown
What waking we must bear before our own.

TO PASSERS-BY

I see you are puzzled in your endless queues
By this most thrilling of all thrilling views
From which your children do not run in fear:
A corpse whose patches of corruption stink
And yet whose eyes, it seems, are proud, and blink.
Believe me, I should speak if you would hear,
But as things are, the facts alone must say
That this glass coffin is my only way:
I am no museum-piece, you pay no fee,
Nor have I any manager but me,
Conditions are my sole publicity...
So if you must file past, your note to make,
Muttering 'Christ crucified! He's not a fake!'
Of malice I bear you none, nor do I bite.
But do I not remind your gaping sight
That you will pay, and not a price you like,
For all the liberties you choose to take?

BLITZENKRIEGER

I woke on top of a lichenous mountain
From what seemed the sweetest sleep. My nostrils quivered
With non-expectation, though the air was sharp;
The sun did not exasperate my stare
In the morning's blue. And long lay I there
In the unthinking calm.
Birdsong enlightened the deserted sky
But still, still I lay, awaiting the silence
When darkness swallowed the ordinary day.

Darkness complete, birds folded in their sleep,
Not peace descended, but from somewhere far below
A cacophonous music surprised my ears,
Whose challenge to their quiet at last aroused me,
Outraged and curious, to scan the valley for its source.

I had not stood long enough on the brink
Even to peer a moment, when agitated men
In whose hands lanterns bobbed up and down nervously
Burst in upon me. One, whom I did not know, silly
In Austrian holiday-dress, seeing me, cried out.
His companions remained in a cautious knot,
But he strode towards me with purposeful respect
Odd in a stranger, his lantern held rudely high;
And when at lackey's distance, looked me in the eye.
Although forebodingly the feather stuck upwards
In his ridiculous, innocent Tyrolese hat,
I paid him regard no more irritably scant
Than his manner seemed to demand. 'You, there!' I said,
Gesturing downwards, 'you must have climbed up from that.
Whose is that music playing now, so cruel and dull?'

He frowned in spongy deference, and white-lashed lids
Reduced the pity of his servant-stare –
But at what plight? 'Why, you, fellow, varlet,' I asked,
Almost touched, 'How does my question trouble you?'
And with tears breaking his guttural harshness, he sobbed:
'Oh, Herr Blitzenkrieger, oh poor dear gentleman,
What can distract you from knowing it's your own?
What grief can have driven you to flee from the performance
In such dishevelled state, alone, and speaking English?'

His sad arm let the lantern fall, and by its light
I gazed at my unadjusted dress: bright-buckled
Shoes of yellow suede, gaiters to match; and bulbous
Baggy billowings of striking stripes – the trousers,
Perhaps? – peach waistcoat fancifully embroidered
With crotchets and quavers and rests; and the jacket,
Enormous, of skin-smooth violet-orange check;
Gravy-spotted blue-maroon cravat...
My hand went to my head – but plucked from curled velvet
Sharply, as if hurt, a single stark grey feather.

I would have run away, but he plucked at my coat,
Its huge arms bulging and flapping – holding me back
In the rising wind. 'Herr Blitzenkrieger! Adolf!
Is it possible you do not remember me?
It is Hans Bübelschzick, your private secretary.
Of all men I alone knew of your private problems:
Your poor distracted wife, your famous compassion –
But Adolf, come back to us, pray, come back to us.
All is now doubly well. The cultured journals
Are informed not only of the subtle brilliance
Of your discord, convinced of the significance
Of your anxious orchestration, so echoing
And shrill, as vital to their understanding of
Both atonality and *dafürhalten*,
But also, my friend, I have sold to them today
Complete with photo and glossy diary facsimile

The splendid story of a fine devotion
To a worthless cause: so now, Master, the world is yours.'

Some power restrained me from the wrong path.
That music was no longer mine! And my voice failed
To speak his unfamiliar tongue. Instead of shame,
I blundered on in astonishment and pride
And left what garments my furious trembling hands
Could pluck away, behind. 'Listen, listen!' he pleaded,
'If it is The Heart again, I am your confidant and friend.
The way you go no cities lie. Oh, think once more:
Remember, your gay rehearsals, the notes both true
And false! Calf-love! The joy of fraternizing
With Europe's greatest thinkers on equal terms:
Those talks, veined with brandy and caffeine, night-long,
With Überstumpfkenhitzel on the Bounds of Mind!
Listen to your Electronic Rhapsody below!
For even while Wacknagel stabs at your atmosphere
With his showy conducting ("it was his chance,"
He moaned aside, "*Der liebe Gott*, this craziness,
It is *der sonnenstich, der seligeit anblick*")
Its daring evocation of unscored confusion
Holds your blond audience, they are swayed and rapt.'
'*Schnell!*' he whispered to a nonchalant subordinate
Among the men who had followed him, '*Der Wein!*
Come, Master, to the *zeitgeist* drink your wine!'

But I had darted from his reach before he spoke.
How fortunate to find this cave nearby
Into whose entrance in a face of sheerest rock —
Apparently a fault — I penetrated.
Knowing me gone — but how? — his respect turned to rage:
He threw a servant's temper, stamped and yelled, and then,
As suddenly, he shrugged the business out of mind, cried '*heil!
Adee!*' and led his little band of men away.

This cave is narrow, dark and cold, with flinty ground —
Not like my waking-place. Here must I stay and sleep
Awhile? Strange that my comfort-loving bones enjoy
Such rockiness. What wonder that their ache demands
So longingly more and yet still crueller beds!
But what of myself? I puzzle: that fool audience.
Oh how may I disenchant their separate selves
Of my naughty music, in the bleak fog of *zeitgeist*?

How, sleepless in my puzzlement, possessed by wonder,
May I discover from them, unnoticers,
What doors and windows it's my task to shut, so long
Left open now? But impossible to keep secret
The madness of my waking.
                    Blitzenkrieger,
Upon this eccentric retirement, all your works
Put out of commission, how now, sir, will you make
Your naked return to that rude slut, of sense bereft,
Whom long ago in ignorance you loved and left?

THE LAST CHANCE
[TO THE PRIME MINISTER]

The prime minister (the man himself, of course)
Had spent many of the least anxious of his
Moments (those away from state affairs that is)
Worrying why my devotion to the cause
Was punctuated by so many lapses –
Thefts, drinking-bouts, absences, disappearances
Into thin air, even (it was reported).
Yet diplomacy had to be supported
By some kind of rotten stuff (he gave a sigh).
You had to condone the ungentlemanly
And be damned to the Club consequences:
Fellows like Nasser do not qualify
After all, for any brand of Old School Tie –
But only the defeated have turned an eye
From the knowing chaps who take the chances.
Still, *why* couldn't the Club circumstances
Separate the confusion from the force?
No doubt about it, my value was immense.
My record: worst in his experience.

But one day in the course of my duties
(Which are cloudy now: to assassinate
An agent in a train, and separate
The P.M., though in the same carriage,
From the possible damning consequences,
I think it was) he heard my wife in a rage
Chasing me through the sliding entrances:
She stamped, screamed, spat, did worse than nag,
And though I'd been drinking to get courage up,
Reduced me in public to a wrung rag.
He knew then my difficulties when working,
And noticed, too, that despite events
The complex murder-task I wasn't shirking.

Lately I took on a routine assignment
To plant a bomb at the docks; but got drunk
And left it at home. Arrived in the marshes

I realized that I ought to do a bunk —
Though I felt quite as splendidly unsunk
As the important ships I hadn't blown up.

Did dishonour finally force my retirement
To look after my own ruined business
In this roofless shack between Grays and Purfleet?
No use asking me why the air smells so sweet:
About all I have here is one cracked cup,
And everywhere else, the hell of a mess.
Something there is to my credit. I spent
My last few bob on a wire to my wife
Promising to restore my shattered life
For love of her, and asking her to wait.

The bomb? Well, it would have been too late
Even if I had remembered; besides,
She wasn't there: it's odd how she decides
Not to be when there's anything funny up.

But this time she made up her mind to make
One of her rare public appearances —
Crazy though! How could she have known where I was?
For just as I was going to demand the sack
Giving the familiar false address
The prime minister (the man himself of course)
Walked gingerly into my tidy shack
And smiling said: 'I think I can say at last
That the Club understands. Your wife came there —
You wouldn't credit what she wanted to know!
Why wouldn't they get you out of this place?
Pay you at least ten thousand a year?
No hint of were they prepared to take you back;
And she spoke to the lot of them as to one face,
Treated them all like servants in disgrace,
And left even the most eminent aghast...
Therefore dear chap, what with the train and that,

We realize now what you've been through –
Your lapses we can forget to excuse.
So, dear boy, and you needn't bother to refuse,
You leave now for a secret training-place
To learn how to be a top diplomat.
Accept all your dud cheques, and this agony-hat,
Presented by the Club, all of whom knew,
One time, what you countlessly endured.
I therefore officially state: We can use
Your talents now we know you're truly cured –
Always provided you get yourself insured.'

'Take your hat to hell!' I said. 'You've had your due.
She speaks to me singly, and she speaks true.
When have I expressed a wish to see you?'

'Now wrap it up' he warned, 'stop taking chances.
Opportunities like this come far and few.
Play up your luck: it was the bitch herself that
Did the trick, dear boy. You can rest assured
That her rage disclosed your circumstances!
Who else could have arranged this interview?'

THE EXECUTION

The big day dawned. They had not told me.
But the warder, cutting the grubby pack
For the last time (I won easily)
Said shyly, 'Me and the boys from the back
Would like to say we'll miss yer. Here mate,
Take what they gave me ter give yer. Yer card.
The public's 'ad theirs. We issued yourn late,
Unofficial like, to make it seem less 'ard.'
For weeks now I'd been waiting for sentence,
The first under new laws which couldn't fail:
Condemned for an undisclosed offence,
But pronounced beyond an undefined pale.
And here at last, some clerk's indelible
Filling the blanks, on a yellow hand-out,
It was: *Beauty is not expendable,*
But we cannot preserve Our Parks without
Economies, therefore prisons will end.
Convicted men will now be set the task
Of Nature-Preservation. Duties depend
On men's degrees of guilt, not what men ask.
Case Number One. Name: Seemore. *Crime:* Extreme.
Task: To the Lions at Regent's Park at Noon.
Bus Route 74, St Pancras Steam,
Or tube Camden Town and walk. *Book soon.*

Bracing myself, I shared the warder's joke.
'That Pierpoint's fretting 'isself sick I bet.
It's a noble death, and better than the rope.
Stroll in natural like, with a cigarette.
Give the crowd their sport and keep on smiling
And you'll go down to 'istory ole pal –
Put up a show an' you'll 'ave 'em whistling
Just like at them Romish martyr chaps an' all.'

I do not remember my last steps,
Except weeping women, kids with ices,
The men dressed up, in their best Sunday caps,
And armed with countless applause-devices;

The clang of the gate, and a huge silence.
Recalling the warder's words (what else to do?)
I lit up and strolled to a sleeping-stone,
Sat down, and crossed my legs. 'Who in hell are you?
I can see that you're no early Christian,'
Growled the lion, almost inaudibly.
'I suppose you'll have to have some of my meat,'
He added, while sniffing at me rudely.
'It's a circus-trick! What a bloody cheat!'
Someone yelled out. 'We want a refund now!'
And while, though still apprehensive, I began
To talk to the lion, and think out how
I'd refuse its stinking offer – to a man,
The crowd started growling themselves, and went
Slowly home, with the new laws disgusted,
And muttering against the government,
Angry, suspicious and disappointed.

FOUND ON A BUILDING SITE

'Dear One:
          I am naked on a building site
In Penge West. It is 1.5 a.m., and cold;
The mist wreathes around me, rising in columns.
I shall have much to think of, but chiefly
What shall I do at dawn?
I am writing this with a piece of coal
On a sheet of a tramp's stained newspaper...
Dum spiro spero: perhaps you will find this
Before the gaunt sirens of daybreak speak.
If not, then think of me, but make no enquiries.'

Thus sometimes the poor spirit.

THE ADMINISTRATORS

In the administration of culture,
Watching our interests, are poetasters
Who wear coloured waistcoats with gold buttons;
Below their suffering countenances,
Like little lights shining upwards
Sometimes perch bright bow ties.
It is to them we owe those long readings
In public places (we are still allowed to miss them)
Those charming speeches from the stage,
Making us feel at home with the right writers –
Half a glass of *vin ordinaire*,
Rind of high-quality cheese, a stone
(We did not even ask for bread) and a few words with
Themselves: for seven-and-six.
All financed by government grant.

They had their careers planned at sixteen
Down to the finest detail: even to
Those unhappy verses on lust at twenty-two
(We all knew
And their wives too
That they'd done a thing or two
At twenty-two):
To the later more resonant odes,
Suggesting development though no loss of potency,
On the warmth and blessings of married love –
How they brought a hint of romance perhaps,
A sense of Man's predicament
To a rare lady's bed;
To the tauter verses of despair:
The agonized song
That the Bomb is wrong
To the last, maturing, comfortable
Swing to the Right.

By the rays of a setting British sun
They sip their old port at thirty-five,
Headily pretending this is life...

Then, sighing as though hidden cameras
Were recording their creative privacy –
The unconscious beauty of their bearing
Of life's contrastingly so crude burden –
For eager audiences of student-sensitives
Whose applause rings in their well-trained ears,
They retire to beautifully appointed studies
('Do not disturb me Penelope.')
To pen longish neat stuff on how they yearn, really,
To give it all up, go back to nature, and so on.
(We should say: 'Dear Aunt: I am looking forward
Very much to my holiday this year.'
But we do not know enough about
The transformations and transmutations of Art.)

When in the act of composition,
They forget carefully the furtive adultery
In Hampstead High Street, that awful business
On the Heath itself (this is too personal –
The Muse prefers the more dishonest lads);
Put out of mind the slightly embarrassing
Writings of dead men who led different lives,
Though trapped on their shelves and sealed
With fullest explanatory annotations;
Ignore most studiously of all
The letters of refusal that they have to write
To those less fortunate but still living
Whose breathing – is it? – somehow halts their pens.

LIVING BY THE RIVER

Nature has left too many relics here.
I lived on what remained of the fresh air;
    Weeds choked development sites
    And not even Human Rights
Could check the river damp. It was unfair.

So my own nature came on, like the rain:
The schoolmaster with his whistle and cane
    Also possessed the Home Life,
    The Garden, the Children, the Wife;
The obstinate and isolated brain.

That day when with bitterness I found
Nothing would grow on my sullen patch of ground
    I felt my life's emptiness,
    The morning's lack of progress,
Paper flowers, the open bed like a wound.

I packed and tried to leave, but soon came home.
They said: 'You can't afford to be alone.
    Do what you like in there,
    But remember what is fair:
Property is theft but the dirt's your own own.'

I knew what they meant (for cleanliness I sigh),
Did all my washing without asking why;
    But cannot decently depart
    Without mastering the art
Of getting clothes hung out by rivers dry.

REQUEST ON THE FIELD

When I was broken down and unemployed
You found me bitter, wry and under-joyed.
I would not pay my licences or dues,
To vote I did improperly refuse.
So captain-like my shoulder-blade you smote
And cried: 'Up lad! Cast off your sullen coat
And (after you have registered your vote)
Get on the pitch among the knaves and fools
And play the game according to their rules –
They're doing, after all, what you won't do.
Respect them then. Later love comes, too.'

I heeded your wise words, and now am on the field
With shirt and socks and red-cross shield.
But before you dribble off, at captain's call,
Could you explain the absence of a ball?

POOR FATSO

Podge (the unloved one in you, even,
Ectomorph: unacknowledged pastry-king
Who muffles your nerves' caterwauling)
Dreams of sherbet and chips in a Turkish den:
Some place all his own, with no other men,
Where plumpened girls swinging their silk hips
Dance at his pleasure in a room of whips;
Whole days and nights to choose one pair of lips;
Ruler of all, without problems of state;
Master, from his puffed couch, of female fate.

Poor Fatso, rolling – like a tear who sheds? –
Down the sad eroded front, seeking fun
From the giggling seaside girls he dreads;
But for his pimples and his nerveless laugh
Disclaimed forever by their casual beds.
Even Fatso (whom you reject, lean one –
Though cushion for your nerves and secret half)
Gives up: by dream-dances blown to shreds.
But in that last explosion, will he change heads?

HISTORY LESSON

For the master who is limiting freedom
History's not like school any more.
They call out death-dates in the still classroom,
Watch motes in the sun, the afternoon
Wear on; listen contentedly, perhaps,
To the chronicle of justified acts.
For him, though, it's not what went before,
But the shut mind planning to condone
What it now understands, is guilty of.
(All slanderers of freedom or love
Plead 'History, not us!' in self-defence:
'Circumstances, not ourselves, make sense!')

The teacher thinks, 'Should I say more?'
But there's no time: the written lesson
Must begin. 'Write,' he says, 'on the reason
For *Either* this *Or* that necessary war.'

He blinks, remembering the same sun,
His free mind in silence
Groping: *'Which war of these, which one, or none?'*
That impulse stifled by an urgent voice
Which he now imitates:
'Choose now! The time is short. You have the facts.'

And of how he felt so coldly un-alone,
Could write nothing but words never his own.

TEA WITH MISS STOCKPORT

Thomas the Wastrel, the Pay-Corps Colonel,
'Retired', and I: all on Wednesdays took tea,
Trapped by charity, in her lacy parlour,
Miss Stockport's. Gingerly always we sipped
From her leaf-thin china, bit delicately
Through her tiny, venerable sandwiches;
Answered with cleared mouth, crumb explosively
Imagined on lip, her smallest questions;
Wiped sweating fingers with frightened secrecy
On the wiry fur of her humped chair-arms
Beneath their starched, white antimacassars.
Yet from her we enjoyed no more than this.
No silver passed. Why, we expected none.

How were we so timid? Out of her presence,
Relaxed at last in the Boilermakers',
Six o'clock striking, we'd guffaw enough,
And mimic her with knowing glee-gurgles –
As if we drank off cash she'd given us,
A burden of alms to laugh off toughly.

We were men with little to commend us:
Thomas in and out (Miss Stockport ignorant?)
A common pimp who left off drink merely
To lounge in stews; the Pay-Corps Colonel
Corrupt, rotten beneath his taut brown skin,
Drummed out for underpaying coolie gangs;
Myself, complicated and cleverer,
A remittance man with parents too poor
To send him farther than this town
From which, in thirteen years, I'd left not once.

What magnet was Miss Stockport that weekly
We were filings in the field of her will?
That Thomas, who'd injured prison-warders,
Could not lie to her face? That the Colonel,
Whose yellow eyes smouldered balefully
With greed, choked shyly on her seed cake?

That I, who loathed religious old ladies,
Shared their embarrassed confusion at tea

The sixty-third Wednesday we were punished enough
For our words, which I swear she never heard.
The tea was bitter, though we dared not complain;
The sandwiches, delicate as ever,
Were filled with a fishy paste, and burned our tongues;
But we munched on, while she sat strangely quiet,
Leaving parish affairs untouched upon
So oddly that we missed the comfort
Of our usual tense and secret boredom.

Pain conquered Thomas first – he who had,
In unfamiliar absence of stubble,
With bladder distended, so often sat tight:
At his stomach grasping, eyes rolling, gasping
'Excuse me, I must wash my hands!' he ran
To the door. The Colonel next, though more stiffly,
Succumbed. 'The toilet, Madam,' groaning, 'my hands!'

I on her sofa collapsed, in fever;
And if what I heard and saw then was a dream,
Of delirium born, I've kept it a secret.
For while men moved in and out, policemen
And surgeons, none seemed to see me lying there,
None but Miss Stockport. Uncovered I lay,
Speechless, but hearing, 'They have passed away';
Witnessing the sympathy of the rector,
And her confident distress.

                    Then, later,
The house empty, my hostess came to me:
'Aha!' she said, 'so you were the chosen.
Now, young man, you must have a thorough wash.'

Her pearly dentures then took sudden root,
Leapt into her gums with maidenly spring;
Her hair from its buns tumbled and scattered,

Flew wild as she kilted her skirts and danced
With flushed and panting speed. Pointing at me,
Skinny finger outstretched, breathless, she said:
'I am your bride, your pain will now subside,
Prepare, prepare, and no longer wonder
Why you visited an old lady from whom
No benefits accrued, whose will was death.'

Of that night, I say nothing. But I left
Next morning, from the back, a different man.
Chastened, I caught an afternoon train
Away from that town at last;
Pale with the strain – chastened, but somehow gay.

Poets, beware of laughter at all ladies.
And mankind, you with the future, watch it.
Not funny Miss Stockport, and not funny,
Either, the shuddering question: What if
We all, going to wash our hands, pass over?

REMINISCENCES OF NORMA
1971

TO SALLY CHILVER

La Pasionaria, *what's permitted?*
What is grace? The communists all want Ben-
Ville Manor. No pasaran. *But they did.*
They do. Oh now what really does go on
In your head (what sadness turned it grey?)
Throughout the purposes-ridden Russian day?
If I did not talk too much I'd listen
To all the things you wisely would not say.

SATIRES

THE INVITATION

Toupée askew after the dusty journey
He stepped blinking out onto the platform
And she was there to greet him.

They had said in the blurb (he wrote it)
'Himself a poet and critic of distinction';
So nice it had been to receive her letters –
Almost unbelievably naïve they were:
'I'll send a photograph so you can recognize me' –
And to be invited to her flatlet
Before lecturing to a local thought-group.

After the photograph he'd indeed taken interest,
With its accompanying note:
'Love in your more than tentative estimation
Is exactly what I too have been searching for;
Men here are coarse in comparison to what you have said;
What Krishnamurti suggests, you are…'
He was rubbing his hands, he could not help it
(Though properly ashamed).

So now, belly held back, with springier step
Than at P.E.N. or Hampstead parties,
He strode down the platform.
'So this is Westcliff…'

And she was even better than he had expected, hanging on to
His every word like an angel.

Soon, with whisky's special sincerity, he was saying:
'The spirit is everything but I have a habit
I have struggled with all my life.
You can talk about it with me. Give me advice.

I think physically, need to discuss
The ethereal significations
Comfortably between sheets, with someone like you.
Whatever happens
It would be different with you.
The contact would scarcely matter.'

Then, when apparently safe in her bathroom,
Having a wash and brush-up before immediate bed-work,
Regumming his wig, whistling with appreciation,
Lower plate riding firmly on the shrunken gum
The door burst open.
Youths,
Reckless and sharp in shiny jackets with emblems, healthy at twenty,

Knocked him down, kicked his soft underbelly;
Stamped on him as if he'd been Coriolanus –
While brazen in her shift she stood and smiled:
'I shall eat these two in a jiffy, Mr Poet.
Take their blows as my advice.
Crawl back to the Smoke. Two can play
At your game – and don't forget it.'

And limping from Fenchurch Street, pubs not yet open,
Clutching his shredded corset,
Hair pocketed in the too-stiff breeze,
He realized that for the first time ever
He was helplessly, generously, forgivingly,
In hopeless love;

And he read with joy in an Essex newspaper how
He had been taken suddenly ill
And Miss Love herself had deputized with a talk on
Aspects of poetry.

QUEEN LEER

Sado-pathic, thanks for drawing
Some madness out of me.
Forgive me now that I am throwing
You through sewers to the sea:
Successful poultices grow more than grey
When hoarded past their one half-day.

CENSOR JACK

In his rare spasms does Censor Jack shout out
The words he rules that we must do without?

SUNDAY MORNING WALK

Trapped as the Church disgorges
Its pollarded congregation
I note the bred not-glance
Of a fascicle, which forges
By variform configuration
Autonomy's *insouciance*,
At an unholy ostentation
(Disciplined intimation
Of next week's battered sermon):
My Russian failure to enhance
Sunday's achromatic orgies
By ritual excoriation
Of my face. Oh Christless ignorance!
Nor does this growth, though getting on for
A *Light-of-the-World*-ish length
Imply the kind of moral strength
That could empty a Church with scourges.
No. But noon's nasty shadow's more
Scissile, when an encumbrance,
Than weeds whose ravages suggest
That beardless integration
Is no remedy at all for plants.

I HAVE NEVER FELT

'I have never felt that there was any inherent virtue in powerful feelings and simplicity, though evidently some poets... Poetry can be honest, I agree, but it has greater duties... it must perform its moral functions... I don't enjoy poems written by... wastrels.'

J. Fuller, *Poetry Society Bulletin 60*, 1969.

Upon men of unfortunately strong emotións,
Moral failings
And vile simplicity
Is ever-fixéd the most baleful, disapproving gaze
Of Fuller, J., versificationist,
And teacher of the young, of Magdalen, Oxenford.

I plead to you: observe unease. You're not enjoyed.
Spit out those siren tears.
Eat your proper bloodless meat
Oh wastrel Mariner:
Life's troubled bubble's broke by John.

When he encounters problems domestic
John's feelings are, I hope, 'not strong':
He life's greater duties knows
And's more agreeable.

May on the public map of Poesy
O rally-hard his driving be:
Directions planned, and navigator-uttered
With superb correctitude;
All watches synchronized, and face
Set in determination quite as strong
As your foul feelings are.

And learn from John, meanwhile, your grief to minimize
Should he not win.

THE CRUEL GRAVY

I used to be a stanzaic boy, conned the porters at Christchurch,
used quaint words, scanned the swans at the edge of the sedge,
pernoctating. Now i am concreto purely, though there were
stages: pour example i had a period cool in streatham i penned
structures for analysis notrelated to my self, a promising
organic persona notexisting a structuremaster from wch big
Wimsatt cd extract i rhymed it big, was winning whn without
warning a friend said that « shatskin » wd be giving a strong
talk at the Penge Ethicallogueinth chair It changed my
*vida*POETRYhesd quotinghis banne d address to the workers
of Omsk / IS THE DIRTYVEST u cast off after labour:
:THAT & MY WIFE'S CON crete knockers/ /endofshatskin
/ I am not read but the freedom of these massesappeals;s.
wentwithaMercedes into the river but had given me the
beginning / SERIOSO mes amis i am now one of you UUU
ChristLogue Spike Jack am out to SHOCK SHOC K i will
use FEAR LESS WORDS mein freud i am bearded now
PERFORM SMELL am in ADVERTISING &my lines
honour MY breathingnotthe sense. That crazy Shakescene
was *projective*plusfield compostit's better now & i can still
astonishingly hv a sherry with dons 'mongst silvertheyto
me listen somewith davy I mopwithbreadpellets up gravy
pity applauding me armpits & i will give you th clothes next
me skin *INTIMATE? goodby!] ½tomlinsong wightman
polyfilled flute]
E

TO ALL WATCHERS OVER PUBLIC MORALITY

Secret dwarf pornographers who live
In your cisterns, repressed gentlemen,
Gaze lewdly at you as you bath.
What a heavy burden you have to carry!
They are yourselves,
The utterances you have banned:
They pen long nasty books and peddle them,
Sure of sale (true offspring of your commission)
In the rusty Paris of the pipes...

Here you get the raw material
From which you learn your duties
To the public. Study them closely
To reach the heart of obscenity:
Long lists of bad words every schoolboy knows
(Read them aloud in the echoing bathroom as relief
To so much protocol);
But most of all pore lovingly over
The luscious glossy series showing
Policemen, truncheon and naked writer...

You more than weekend in dirt.

A VERSIFIER IN PRIVATE
to Poets in Public

Dangerous in my Y-fronts
To thin-legged Harrods cousins,
Sometimes I also simulate
Evenings of undefeat.
Passing my Churchill memoirs
And well bound great editions
My six suits half in mind
And the Jermyn shirts
I bear to my roseate terrace
A careful gin
And to you Leonardina show
Although you are common
An old romance
En vers surfin, parfumé,
Telling of how once, in the unkempt world,
An imprudence flicked
With stroboscopic speed.
In its lines I celebrate
That *momentito.*
But once is enough; oh never allow
Life to seep out of
The all-inclusive filing cabinet.
Fetch me my gross of condoms,
But first: fellate.
I shall put out of mind your servitude,
Let it be lost in your deglutition. But
Leonardina, I shall not be involved.
I never propose:
My concinnous spurt dissolves
All fears and loves:
I am married to death.

THREE IMITATIONS

FEDERICO GARCIA LORCA:
1910 (INTERVAL)

Those eyes of mine in nineteen-ten
did not see the dead buried
nor the dawn-weeper's celebration of ashes
nor the trembling heart, stranded as a sea-horse.

Those eyes of mine in nineteen-ten
saw the white wall where the little girls pissed,
the bull's mouth, the toadstool
and the secret moon which in corners lit
scraps of dry lemon in bottles' hard shadows.

Those eyes of mine! in the horse's collar;
in sleeping Santa Rosa's tortured breast,
in the roofs of love – with groaning and cool hands –
in a garden where frogs ate cats.

The attic where old dust gathers statues and moss,
boxes which store the silence of eaten crabs,
in the room where the dream came true.
My little eyes are there.

Ask me nothing. I know now that lives
when they seek out their course, meet their void:
a tragedy of leaks in unpeopled air
and in my eyes the children are dressed, not bare!

UMBERTO SABA: WINTER NOON
[Mezzogiorno d'inverno]

Just when I was still contented
(God pardon me for having said
Such a vast, appalling word), who swept
My curt joy away, so that I nearly wept?
You might say, 'A certain lovely girl
Walked past you there, gave you a smile'
– But it was a balloon, a balloon
That floated, blue against sky-blue,
When my heaven had never been so bright
As at that clear, cold winter noon:
A heaven of clouds, small and white,
Of windows blazing in sunlight,
Thin smoke from a chimney or two;
And over the scene, the divine scene,
That globe which had slipped loose
From the hand of a boy who'd been
Heedless (surely he shed some loud
Tears, in the middle of the huge crowd,
For his sorrow, his enormous sorrow,
At losing his toy?).
Between the Square and the cafe
I sat in wonder watching
At how it now rose, now fell – his joy.

FERNANDO PESSOA: POETS
[Autopsicografia]

Poets pretend
They pretend so well
They even pretend
They suffer what they suffer.

But their readers feel
Not the pain that pretends
Nor the pain that is
But only their own: that's real.

And so upon toy rails
Circling reason like an art
Runs round the model train
That's known by the name of heart.

REMINISCENCES OF NORMA

1

I smooth out a map of where I live,
Run my finger along your street,
Feel your will in the fibre of the sheet;
But remember you said, 'I hate home:
It is so far to come';
And wishing to spare you, even in my
Helpless thoughts, from dwelling again here,
My eyes roam to the surrounding district –
Quiet villages you might have visited
In sad escape; or to which, in a dream-life,
We might have gone. But my life's not full enough
For me boldly to know such other places...
Defeated, I put away the map.
Find it has a cutting edge:
Has become, with the sharpness
Of your mastery, cold, and cruel.

2

It is well for you tonight pretty girl
To put on your dancing stockings and twirl twirl
In exquisite clubs of drink and lust
While I rack myself with jealous thoughts
Of brute sailors smirking
And your crushed self finding in their tattooed arms
More sweetness than in my foolish love.

Or perhaps an ambitious clerk,
The facets of his face gleaming in subdued light
Is at this moment subjecting you
To an expensive obscene ritual
From which your joy in his concentration
(Which excludes you completely),
Excludes your lover.

Or perhaps you are seducing someone comically,
Whom 'you quite like really', in a taxi:
A sick columnist who lives on pills
And celebrates, rolling naked to Wagner,
The supremacy of white rulers.

Or perhaps in teenage coffee-bars
With black discs in front of your eyes
You are committing welfare;
Yearning later to taste their contempt
And to be robbed of your awful love –
A mystery in which your lover has no share.

So in my imagined bitterness,
I, who have no rights over you whatever,
And who abuse you with such thoughts,
Jealously writhe.

Yet how can I believe
That when you take down your hair
And come to me smiling
Your heart is not there?

3

The new girl with violent hair
Ignored me daily on the stair
Her glance-away was like a stare
        I make my own disasters

Across the sky I saw her hand
A bundle into a waiting hand
I wanted not to understand

Parcelled cock to be sacrificed
To a God who'll take away a life
I had not known could be sacrificed

She went down a darkening street
With a knife to make my last defeat
Who was she going that night to meet

I lay in wait for my own death
Expecting to hear my final breath
I dreamt and watched them plan my death

I saw them work at their Black Arts
Hated their understanding hearts
In the temple where death starts

But when I woke this vision cleared
I looked for the new girl whom I'd feared
The death was that she'd disappeared

Have you seen a hole in emptiness
Where nothing was have you seen less
When you feared death have you been death
                        You make your own disasters

4

Pasty, with brazen curls, you dream away
Your captain day:
Unblossoming you shed your right to pray.

I canker you, my bore and stride
Are cruel. Writhed in your side
I see your other face, in patience skied...

As I am sickness, so you are my rose:
Even what is dying grows, and grows.
What will be what I lose

But one larger rosebud to explore?
But I promised before
Kindness, the sunned quiet of a slow shore,

Patience like yours. Then give me now,
Make me demand, that sharp rosary
To count for you, to clack endlessly
Your general time away;
Oh let me beg, cocoon at last, to be
Your sadder suffering face below –
Loathed in my lair, so skilled and grey.
By counting your scentless beads in such a way

Might not I then become
The whole true tree of you, and dragon home?

5

Come with me to Heligoland. It's now
A wilderness, I think. Was bombed so often
That there's nothing there...

Where is it then? you ask.
                              Do not tease me with your map.
It would be new in this way, that there are
No night-clubs, no chance bars
Where I might embitter myself, falling
Into soft new company.

There are birds maybe; and in my dreams of you
Might be love-avoided-as-it-should-be:
The thing not in eyeshot, the lived-in beauty.

Do not wonder that now
I drum my heels against the timbers
Of a narrow passage, suspended from a hook.
This is no game I play in place of metaphor:
Remember your joking hand so long ago
That hoisted me from ground too hard to bear,
To this lowest hook my folly could hang me by?
Now I wish to celebrate you
In most barren Heligoland, where nothing's for pleasure.

For beneath my feet, to rest them,
You place volumes of poetry
Who do not care for poetry.

6

Yesterday I took you to a place
And waited in the car. Now lying here in bed
I am still there: cannot remember
Returning ever. When memory fails
Today is bled, yesterday fed.
In the night with trees around I am afraid.
Let me get out of this.
What is Norma's face
And why's
The house she entered locked?
Sitting in the car's being nowhere;
Late and alone, no breath, I think no thought;
Look down at the hole in my chest, no pain, just a lump of
Blood-ice.

Many lives have I such:
Of terror – and perhaps
Sweetness indescribable?
In one I sit here, not-dead –
But in one more, amazed,
Am warm and saved.
Too much too much!
Not strange I twitching inhabit
A greyness of brains racked,
Remember not to forget.

7

I met you, Norma, dearly young,
In scented night. Though you spoke of wars
Between men and women, of alternate triumphs,

I noticed the trees only, ghostly-green
In dark. Your youth excited my mind,
My eyes were fixed, I did not dare to think
So much for your embrace I longed.
You were so fair
You would not lead me home until sun shone.

The flies were busy round desire
Before you drew me in. I eyed
The crossed dildoes on your walls,
The sex-stained trophies
The splendid images of death;
In my own first gruntings heard the buzzings of decay
On the tender face of that amorous day;
Wanted to stay.

I tried to be decent in our sty;
Found pleasure gave
Sense back to my eye:
While you lolled into rest
I saw that you were older than I thought
And knew you as a witherer of green,
Obscene
And rotting Helen of all wars never won.
Yet for passion I strained on:
Your stench was that of the divine.

Now you are silent I miss your mind,
Lack the stink of your vanished rind.
Oh how long in your palace will I lust alone
For bones whose flesh so long ago I wronged?

8

Bring Norma
             was a phrase I overheard
Put me in danger. Nothing to do with me;

But John and she did arrive in my mind's
Small cliff-perched house, cut off,
In sneering wind. Below,
The slow sea like a shapeless serpent stirred
In changing blue.
Alone for a moment, as in a fantasy…
Not right of course but I thought: Oh
I want you too. Then John was dead.
We watched his body fall towards the sea.
Then murder made my sex-dreams real.
They come me now to choke, with their white hood
Put on my head.

This is not true, nor was she real, and yet
I am condemned, a felon in a net,
Nor can wake.

9

'One of the best of a valuable series…'
I get bored, love, although of course it's interesting and, true;
Yes love I know that while
On helpful exegeses, dry, of hot desire
I work, you sit there still
Though I no longer quite believe in you –
Now I am so bland may not you strike
And shall I have have have
The old entire, despiséd dream?
Cor!

Nerves would be shot, I should be ill,
Flesh like you might seem.
It's true that strange
Breasts are marvellous meat
But do be wiser lust –
And you, word, in your seat,
You Norma you
Are mostly ghost.

10

Goodbye common history
                    there is no name
I can give that she
                    but yours
Norma
Wife-figure? Ma? This is a photoplay in which
I do not I hope participate
                    Actress, you,
Sweet in the part, so appealing, true

The theme? Some horrible actions in a park:
Worse than sex-deaths, never-seen;
An old man made appearance
On dusks of murder-nights,
Was seen through railings in the mist,
Seemed made half of stone; and half of silence

Then horror. Next night you whom we trust,
So kind, so lovable
An early Anna Neagle in an X! —
Are seen there, thighs
Tempting in the grey, a hint of breasts, but
Face softish stone spilling reckless flesh

That was not I! Sweetly said to my relief
My poor father must not seem to be
The one whose victims die. It was for him.
So noble are you, in this plot, until

I wake to find a face, half flesh and half decay
Turning to stone: this must be the dream. I say:
This is not true, Oh this is just the play

There is no play

11

No vows these days
Or wine of love-praise:
We let friendship freeze
Our old intensities.
It seemed good to be
Not in love but happy:
No lies said,
Friends in bed.
But at the heart of lust
Death pissed.
What seems fragrant
Becomes rank.
And so one look today
Made by you in play
Took my smile away.
Through our soft ease
I saw my end:
The plot, the serious men,
The one absent,
The grave open.

12

I left you Norma and you died alone
In that room whose ancient pieces stopped the sun.
Then from the street towards you there crept one
To wash your body lying on our dark bed:
To sponge your thighs still filthy with my sperm
And kiss pale lips that once were red and firm.
It was the ghost of me who grieving left
At dusk: my Christ-half's turn of cheek away
From me. I could not refuse its gift

And all my lightness now is filled with pain:
As you rise in my mind, so lusty and so gay.
I left you once, but now be mine to hold,
For memory warms what only real is cold!

13

This little love-God is a shit, brown-suited,
Franco-faced, and only He knows if He knows
How He awoke to find Himself i/c affairs
Or how I found myself a witness to
His dull committee. That's what the heart
Of passion's like: a group of psycho-clerks
Considering erections' powers to lie.
Let those who love divinely see the files.

But Norma, you were there, glasses and bad clothes,
Docilely bringing papers to their sides,
Your breasts in satin, peacock-blue,
And my romantic passion was, to penetrate
The centre of your secretarial art:
Love like that aches to know what it knows only,
Or is unknowable. Our sex stank everywhere,
My words were not my own, I envied the grey God-man
Who'd had you once or twice, you tart.

Not you nor God nor His cold secretariat
Can know my journey, not of miles,
To find in nothingness the love I can.

OTHER POEMS

MISTRAL

She went out, for a moment, she said –
    But he lay down in the wind,
Asked it to tell him what loss it was bringing;
    And their son cried 'My father is dead.'
But he with staring eyes still lay, and ringing
The wind made words on the bells
      Which spoke in his head:
        'Tell your son that his mother has sinned
        And his father is dead.'

She stooped to him, stroked him, 'Oh do not lie there
    In the wind, come in by the fire,
The bells speak lies to part us,
      Come in from there.' But she fled in fear;
And the bells rang thus:
'He will not rise, he will not rise, unless she tells
      Where she goes in the Mistral, where,
      And the story of her whole desire
      For the wind in her hair.'

The air became still, and the words he had heard
    Became her surprise:
'Where have I been that my breath
    Comes so fast? Has the Mistral stirred
The bells to speak of death?
The wind is winged and beaked, it taps on the bells
    Always a lying word.
My son, why with such frightened eyes
    Do you stare at me, as if you realise
    That I myself am the Mistral-bird?'

THE BLUE TRUMPETER

Privately to you and while confined
In the jacket of strait circumstance
I smuggle this crude message.

Forgive me free friend if I have stifled
Your unwitting music. Demands of business
Or, I might say, all of earth's beauties,
Will perish at doom. But what is doom?

Even to me, most humble and rejected,
Dreams try to speak. But the strict mind
Censors their message. Thus 'I am alone'
Is vague at too-considered morning,
Shrugged off like an astrologer's warning.
But the message lies within: I signed
By my birth a charter saying
There are Wrongs as well as Rights of Man.

Knowing you were a master of insurance
I left you coolly. Only my dream said
That I returned in afternoon, as a
Blue trumpeter. It was not as myself,
But as a marvellous warrior, famed and scarred,
The hero only I had thought of:
So alive and throbbing white, but with
Blue spots breathing decay. Yes, like this I
Turned up in your pleasant summer garden.

'You are meant to be away, spectre,'
You said, 'but since you are here, I stand you.'
And grinning horribly, to your wife's dismay,
You warned the huge world: 'Come boy, sound that horn!'
'I am here,' I said, 'in a dream merely:

But outside this foolish sleep
I have been here, a winged officer
Of fatal interest. And you have said
"Look, look at this masterful peaked creature
With griffin-wings! He asks impossibilities!" '
(Yes, free friend. My spite to you was myth.
You live in wider gardens now. I beg
You think of all my strictures on you as
Pseudonymous – the naked angel who,
By truth's command, your life made harsh and vile.)

So I made a strange, unearthly music.
Not one understood. And as I played
(Spotted with blue decay in your garden)
I began to wake. All meaning of this dream
Receded from me. But I remember
(Oddly in a mad dream)
How from unknown dells and hidden waters
Herons rose, and veered.

PATHETIQUE

Early fell to the spell of
What wrong have I done love?
Wondered with you how
Gracefully not to allow
Sense a way. Did not know
Flesh has its mind, of danger,
Whose coolness is anger.
Oh why does peace have to end?
At the blue window
Heard the hoarse fulsome call,
Saw the faceless shadow
Of you now know.

THE ANSWER

Why live at all? Absurd question.
Do not ask it. I heard
One say those words, most bitterly,
The heat of circumstance
Stifling a too-guarded mind.
Discovered it was I. Went out,
Determined in the biting day,
To kill all trace of sense. Found
Curiosity too quick; returned
To starker warmth: a naked mind.

SAXELBY

I was asked to compile a Dictionary
Of Names and Places in the Works of Thomas Hardy;
Was pleased at the financial opportunity –
But found the job had been done already
Sometime earlier in the century
By a man called Saxelby.

What a dull man, I thought meanly
(Though told he did it excellently)
Actually to compile a whole Dictionary
Of Names and Places in the Works of Thomas Hardy!

Yet how can I say with certainty
That, victim of terrible vices, Saxelby,
Crippled with alimony,
Pressed by mistresses and penury,
Tensely, angrily, in a drunken frenzy,
Slogging down the busless Dorset lanes disgustedly,
Did not do it only for the money?

IN THE MARKET-PLACE

Half-heartedly at noon in the market-place,
For the thousand-and-first time, I step forward
To assert my sovereignty. Persons, gathered
To see the King my father, ignore me. Then
The usual sneer goes up: 'It's the heir again
Making his claims!' Nevertheless, while the worst —
The thieves and lunatics and hopeless cases —
Bow slobbering at my feet, the people stay:
Something to expostulate upon at lunch
If my father does not pass this way today.

But I maintain a new silence. I dismiss
My crazy disciples, join the mob itself,
Become one of them (unrecognised of course),
Chat pityingly to them of the mad heir,
Mocking him thus: 'He's silent today, praying
To himself for yet further powers and glories.
I knew him once.'

PINCHBECK

Pinchbeck, constructor of automata and other desiderata,
Inventor of the mixture of copper and zinc that bears your
name

(Whose second son and namesake Christopher
Manufactured astronomical clocks, automatic pneumatic brakes
and patent candle-snuffers),
How many of the minikin-frenzied, parchment-faced, task-
rapt, time-pressed
Acquisitive master-jewellers who now so idly cry to cowed
apprentices
'Hand up the pinchbeck!'
Pause to bless your brilliant vital alloy
Of base metals counterfeiting gold
Or care for your soul
Or actualize
That very darkest moment
When crossed in love and heedless on the edge of an
eclipsing scandal
You head-in-hands were driven to sob: 'What is it all for?
What can I care for any more?'

Only then could hopeless red-rimmed eyes when blankly raised
discover
An alchemy that never had been more than casual
So triumphing in the retort
It made you as forgetful of your private pains
As jewellers now are careless of them in their gains.

AN OBSERVATION FOR UNVERIFIABLE
RECONSIDERATION IN A GAME PERHAPS

The preliminaries to your death are
This and that: shaving, a little anger,
Pat the cat's head, write a boring letter.
Your logic can show you nothing better.

Or have in your case fantasies of love
Interfered in a serious manner?
Then we have a false though common basis
Upon which to found a 'friendship' (say)
(Or if I am a lady then you may
Express yourself in a quite different way).

Put this at its very least attractive —
You must admit that on the whole it is,
From routine deathwards-going, a holiday.
Freddy can't have all analysis, no play.

Remember, then, next time your mind must curse
This godless accidental universe,
That only lies prevent it from being worse.

THE CELLAR

The monuments had gone.
Scrolls of their stone
Floated paper-light,
Scattered, settled,
On the ended world
When I saw him first,
Black, without pity.
I am dying, he said,
I shall soon be dead.

Love is death, he said,
As he led into my known,
Needed tomb;
But you did not know,
You spoke it so;
I am dying, he said,
I shall soon be dead.

In ripening dusk I saw
Blood fall from his wound
As down steps and steeper steps
He bled.
Felt in my stiffening side
New lips, the ooze of blood.
I am your father? he mocked.
And he thrust his swelling black tongue
Between my lips as I choked
Nigger, jew, queer!

Your chamber of horrors, he said,
Opening a lost door.
Your key, he said, I am dying.
Feed your wound, lock yourself in.

You'll find her there.
I knew her, but from nowhere,
Knew the two tables there,

The two pens laid;
The paper made of stone.

I need to find what you have,
For I am kind;
I need to find what you have not,
For I am cruel.
I spoke only through my side
Despite my head's despair;
Mouth could not ask, What spear?
I turned the key inside.
Went to her there.
She swung an axe at me,
Its blade swept my hair
As she swung it up there.

I am skull and skin, flesh and hair,
She said, but I am not dead.
They are dead up there.
Nothing living flies in the air,
Nothing living inhabits the earth,
The caves are empty,
But we are living, locked here.
And when I called out, Father,
Father, God the Father,
No one soothed with there there:
I heard only his blood
Drip on the stair.

I look at the walls like dark lakes,
Tall pillars no movement shakes;
I search in vain for the source of the light.
We must, she says, record all thought,
Describe our feelings as we fight –
Until what time! I ask –
Until a time that you have bought.
I can write only, Will this wound heal
Or shall I bleed to death?

She hides her writing with her hand,
Makes signs I do not understand,
Smiles at a thought.
My wound dreams of its food,
I cannot write as I should

And the sound her pen makes
Is like the hissing of snakes.

WHY

Do I cause you to do this? Or is it
A thing clear to you, but strange?
Weather, perhaps, or the change
Of seasons? We stand in fields
And share the bleakness of an Autumn day.
I feel the new chill like comfort,
You knowing yourself, but seeming to give
All your knowledge to me – or to the day?

'How can it end again?' I ask;
But when dusk ends, and when we sit,
I think contentedly,
By the fire, you spread hands like wings:
'I am leaving you for ever.
When I return, I shall have changed.'
And if you become a bird that sings
I have to love a song I do not understand.

Oh vast and vanishing accuser,
So loving as you fly,
Through all Autumns my 'why?'
Echoes, and through all such days
As those you have been with me on.
All of them are questions
Asking, in their similitude,
Where is she now? Where did she go?

Yet did I not hear her say
'Those who truly love are not of your day
Nor can they tell of where they go
Or of how you cannot let them stay'?

TO MISS PARFITT (1934) SADLY:
THIS POEM ABOUT DYING

I've had too much trouble in my life.
Why, writing those words, I went back to
An ancient kindergarten cursive.
When I cried I could not do it
Soft-breasted woolly-warm Miss Parfitt
Took me on her lap. (Now I can,
And anyway, she's old.) Yes! I want
To get away from life, say nothing of
The young magus, the all-intelligent hag
Or the demands of universal love;
There is the darkness in myself
Which for too long I've said was
Not honest to hide. Let me have less
Trouble, is what I ask...

And so you, to whom I have always to speak,
Say with the smile I put on strict lips
'There'll be no poems, no answers,
No harrowing of hell without
The pain you know you want.'

I know I'm speaking to you Adversary.
Must.
Let me as usual put the sentence,
In your mouth: 'For trouble you've got
Your less and less obscure aches hinting
At dying. You always have your dying;
The wish is permanent.'

But need that be trouble?

It's what I wait for, wanting
To know.

GIRL'S SONG

Mr Tropayoz,
Do you trim our fates,
Vendor of goodies and God?
The children love
Your white push-cart,
But your azure sweets
Burn with an icy flame
In the knowing hearts
Of lonely child and lover
Who fear tales
Of the thundering beard
That wags at hell
When you mouth the Word.

Oh monstrous heavens of my blue eyes
Let the stars in them
Trick you into another love:
If then I let you tumble me
Will you change your too vast ways,
Check the divine threat, sweetheart,
For a season be strictly mine,
So that the hopeless people,
Long threatened by your sternness,
May dreamlessly join hands
To dance and sing
'What holy changes,
What nearer distances!'?

THE WORDS

That hag with you there
Has such intelligence
You slit her tongue.
Keep her by you,
Don't be alone
Or search for other
Companions now:
She plays cards better
Than you in your patience
And by not saying
She is not what she is
Startles your care:
What lucky wildness –
Look. You've destroyed
What might have come out!
Patience in you
Is a game for two
And the game is cruel
For it cannot end
Because it must end
When her sewn member,
Which cannot speak,
Wags words through a shriek.

SPEECH FROM A PLAY

Helljoy. When I remark or leer, your eyes
Turn from me, wish neither to curb nor to advise
My different sidle-up from yours, my shut
Grave veering towards the green of life. So lamps
Hung out by you dot all my darkness here:
Thus, if I see a deep green floodlit somewhere,
Which tempts my heart, you frame urgent laws
And having checked me, analyse the cause...
Or else it was some tricked-up garden of your own —
A painted cloth explorable by eyes alone.
I am your subject still. All my paths are cut;
None of my letters travels without stamps.
But while you meet to swearing ban the sea
Or hold committees none of you must miss
You'll think of me: I do not mutter emptily
In these deserted streets: *I'll get you for this.*

QUESTIONS BEFORE PARTING

Have you been the victim of a mistake?
Am I dismissed? At noon I must leave
For Gollemburg, from thence entraining
To the University at Wiesenbahr.
When honourably I've acquired my scar
I shall, like other players, stroll aimless,
Cane hung like a sword from twirling fingers,
As symbol of controlled and practised hate
Along the promenades of Europe's spas –
Building the grim legend of one whose skill
In love and death were equalled only
By his heroic and concealed despair.
The object is: you'll hear. Perhaps I'll come
To you, an errant visitor, drink all
Your whisky, go to sleep on your divan.
Will you say you remember me?

But at this moment, as the time draws near
For my departure, it would be easier
To distract your gaze from birds wheeling
In hundreds against a washed-out sky
By rolling my eyes, gesticulating
In a dying agony (look at me now!)
Than to tell you, as I watch your pale lips,
Face grave in its frame of hair,
That I wish you to say
'I must come with you, even to Gollemburg,'
So that I could answer with a new smile
'You have asked to come with me, so now
I can stay.'

IN MEMORIAM
Brian Higgins
1930-1965

I sit wanting
You to come in
Remembering
How many times
I turned you out
Busy with stuff
On 'books and life'
Or teaching Arabs
About how to use
Short sentences
(Of which you proved
The better master)
And regretting
I thus betrayed
Your need and trust
But knowing you
Understood
Until with all
Guilt assuaged
Bored with my grief
I read the words
Of poems you wrote
And you are here,
No northern ghost
But my friend still
In your own voice.

BEACH, 1737

Beach, poetical Wrexham wine-merchant,
Your *Eugenio* was unremembered
(Despite the dedication to Pope,
The kindly letter from Jonathan Swift)
From the day it appeared, until this moment.
That year, you cut your throat, suffering
From 'a terrible disorder of the head';
But doubtless you knew a fine rescuing Margoose
Before madness finally had you dead.

Hero, now, of one man's melancholy day:
For you I sheath and dispose the keen carver,
Shut all scissors dangerously open,
Coil and neatly tie the hanging rope,
Begging that if darkness must press on me
And serenity quite withdraw its gift,
I shall lie still, and not become madder —
Rising frenetically up to reach
For the knives I have so quietly put away,
Or rushing to dance in the tempting noose.

But your death had its victory, Beach:
Who now can be sure if the bladed sliver
Not yet smashed out of his perfect windscreen,
The high step crumbling on his sturdy ladder,
The death-claw in his excellent machine,
Are not secret wishes, sharply to end
A peace that sanities merely pretend?

TUTHILL'S ENORMITIES

Through disaster I turn poet monthly
Until your shocked charity redeems me,
Pushing clean despair a step enough away.
A packet from England arrived today
By your kindness, with the usual remittance.
Again I burn all. How many foul true odes
Have thus by generosity been checked?

It's quiet here. On some late evenings
The clouds glow like an orange at High Table
In a silver dish. I have some studies
Of God, who knows how every sparrow falls,
To which to apply my too bored intellect.
With no cash, no influence, I share your view
That I can never again be seen by you.
Not many will ever want to solve
The mystery, *What happened to Tuthill?*

I want now only to give my thanks to Gray,
Tell simply what the burnt odes tried to say:
That I loved best one summer afternoon,
A clean-limbed boy, to whom I'd passed all things
On loveliness that my correctitude
Could bear. But while I spoke of ancient codes
Of classic perfection, the glory of Greece,

Of the gentlest ways to wisdom and peace,
My hand, it seemed like God's, sought out
Despair. Just in that private minute
I could believe that lust and virtue mixed,
That hell and heaven by love are fixed.

Here by your leave, waiting for distant death,
I could have a boy, no question asked,
Could laugh at what you miss in Cambridge,
And send the cynical ones a greeting;
Exchange vile letters, though never meeting.
Why instead should memory shake my foolish frame
With unholy contradictions?
Still timid, I drink wine in careful measures,
Maintain a dignity where no one cares,
Give my desires no hell-won rein:
Remember only shared sunlight, friendship,
The womanless fields beneath the arched blue sky,
And the sweetness of my truest lie
Breathed through the first and ultimate kiss:
'It's always innocent, just like this!'

IN THE HOTEL

I climbed to the Fifth up the dangerous tube
Footstraps dissolving The friendly dancer
Went off at a tangent safely where her floor led
I called *This is not my herringbone coat*
Folded it gave it to her to return
To the man who'd placed it on my shoulders like a cloak.

Then climbing was easier.

Back on the Ground
    Sitting in bed with my mother-wife
          You

My wife came in with a double toy-house
One side acid
    the other sweetmeats
And you offered me my mummified self
Which swallowed, I woke

THE SHORE

Somewhere great life streams choicelessly
Beneath the indifferent, cheerful sun;
But wisely I am here, on a grief-dark shore,
Where fishes in cold sand rot saltily
And uncertain nature pullulates
Gently towards its origin, the sea —
Defeating its preservative
To seek sure, spiritless eternity.

My head is sick, hands deathwards reach.
But despair, hope's wine that ripened
In sun that shone here once before,
Mars carelessly the eager quest.

Even these numb gulpings of oblivion
Are uneasy, and drunkenly transform
The ignorant metaphor.

WILDERNESS 1994

To My Wife

WILDERNESS

Sweetheart, remember those small hours when time's
So infinitely stretched: a web so delicate
That only icicles define its baneful density?
It's freezing tonight, no fire will keep
Me warm and I so long for you
That my need to hear your voice, that music
Which turns the ugly and the false back into the true —
My need to hear it aches back into the deep
Memory of what I know you know: those small
                              hours when time's
So infinitely stretched: a web so delicate
That only icicles define its baneful density...

Since my loving begs you to lie absent and
Indifferent to my solitude, for God's mercy
Instruct me in another music: one
Whose shy power transmutes, as your heart can,
This littered and insomniac wilderness
Into a grey-blue lacustrine paradise
As quickening and as placid as your eyes.

THE LONELY GHOST

My mind created you as I emerged
From a blood-flecked dream. And now I'm sad:
I can't destroy you and, you see,
Your good Sundays stopped in Forty Six
And all the years since then, you've been alone
And mourning for those afternoons. In that year
What I most clearly saw was from an army train:
A meagre patch of ground. Let me be there alone I said
Rather than be here. And I was crying inside.

But that year you had Roy and Janice and Bea
If only Sundays. You remember the C Sharp Minor
Best with a click; and heads flung on the sofa-back
For Tchaiko's Fourth all passionate and sweet
With Disney trills, the London traffic 'maimed
By the sad-eyed Russian's marvellous art', you said.
Then just a few small changes. Nothing much.
Like Janice died and Roy went off to Barrow
And Bea just faded out you don't know where; God's
Finger adjusting his stereo balance.
And so you lost all that, and have lived friendless,
Broken, threw all your seventy-eights away.
But as you walk this damnéd world your head
Explodes with noise. Long see I haunting me
Blood dancing to the discord in your eyes.

I will go back to dwell upon that patch of ground.

NORTH

There are some no times
In age's north
When you can be at one
With your younger face
Gazing at firs-distant
North.
I remember my first play:
SEEN: AN EROPLAIN.
Enter: The King and Queen
Aloan.
They were flying North.

OBSTACLES

Between us, the summer evening,
And the maudlin roses of neighbours
Who once were very old, and now are dead:
That contemplation, that memory
Shared to break
Our grief of nerves,
Our soured and heartless days.
Ice on the warm grass,
Magic before our eyes.
A burst of feeling,
A sliver of desire.
Ruin's fascination,
Or fantasy of heartless days?
We are as dry and thin
As roseless sand;
But shall we, human,
Dare to go to bed?
The ice on the grass has turned
To a damp bleb.

INFLUENZAL

Reaching hear watch wind
Disaster threatens but ¿will, will,
By restful telephone dark blue
Be staved? – Noyesno.
By smoking stupefied
With acromycin so
Unalert
From ¿fingered pipe what tunes may flow?
Watch dirty window
Wind's immeasurably low
May not even blow
Fail to think ¿What do things mean?
¡When windless wind is green is green!
Slip into sleep maybe
That visitor will come
As to the good Machado
On edge of dream
'Come with me to see the soul'
Hushed heart-stroked say
'With you alway'
And go
Through hugely vacant halls
Hear rustle of her spotless robe
Feel her soft pulse of almost endless woe.

I WAS A YOUNG MAN ONCE

I was a young man once
Never was one such;
Nose-flute, shoulder-bird,
I lived
In a water-wheel
And heard no music
But my own.

Why did I not fire
That jewelled gun I had
To end it all?
My story'd have been pretty then.
But now I have to add
To those old fantasies
Another's tale.

UNSMILING

Dank. Our shared world shattered, ended.
Yet how can I not look out
At the twilit, unkempt, half-derelict
Garden where once I stood, your arm in mine,
Planning its perfection?

Let it all rot down, like hope.

A single bird sings in the Sunday quiet
As ignorant of lies as of your pain.
The cat rolls. And in my bitterness at this
Edge I'm on, of absolute extinction
(A dangerous place, swarming with fears),
Even as I contemplate finality
I cannot help, so terrible is hope,
Asking if our world could stop. Might not
Its essence be in some laugh: even as a knife
Slashes a throat, in a clean end?
Let Saturn choose, stern and beguiling,
That I may know the sense of its smiling.

TO MY WIFE IN HOSPITAL

You asked me, 'do you still love me?'
I froze, could say only, stiff-lipped
'Why, of course.'

I wish you'd ask this silence in the house,
This hopelessness of music,
This drizzle in our garden.

Two people who were very old
Once loved each other so much
That a god decreed
That they should die at the same time
And become one tree.

Why can't we be such a tree,
Not dead,
Looked at by us together in a past
That not even the worst disaster takes:
That old tree in the valley in Umbria
On which the sun shines
And which thunder shakes?

For long we looked down on it.
Do you remember? But we didn't walk
The long hot way to get to it:
Would we ever be able to pick it out
When we came near to it? Anyway, it was

Too far, *really*,
We said.

A SCRAP OF MOONLIGHT

Walked in the rain to post you a letter.
You, who won't see me, you are so sick and sad.
Wanted at last to be simple, had
Need to speak straightforwardly at last.
So I said aloud in the dusk-drizzle: 'I
Love You' but dismissed it as prosy chatter,
An exhibitionistic matter;
Regressed to the over-complex past,
In which mind ruled heart, and Thou wert ruled by I,
Feelings always tainted by some some half-lie.
Gave up: the trash of governments,
Ferocious fanatics fighting without sense,
The mephitis of the incruciated
Fribble turned to demonic scold;
All the poor, tormented, excruciated,
All the newly demented, love-robbed old...
That at least seemed reason to be bitter...

No excuse. Nothing of that in me not bad.
Drawn *immer schlimmer* from the indignatory
Sewer – no more to it than love-torn litter
Or some man who says of Mercy: 'Plan it!'

Sat in the darkness here, knew this, uneasily
Lamented the gap between false and true,
How I, how we, could ever span it.

Then, as the Moon sailed out and into view
Saw the uninfected fact of you,
Your renewal rinsed of my self-love:
Could hope at last, with no bitterness,
For love in everyone – and knew that meant me, too.

CHRYSANTHEMUMS

Everybody's chrysanthemums,
Everybody's,
Are a good dream that will come true.
And you know as I know
From their sombre colours
Staunch against the heart-withering,
Calamitous, mind-shrinking, encumbering,
Deadening, torturing
Bleakness of weather,
That all true dreams enable,
Enable,
Love to break through.
Look now at the trees,
Stripped as if dead,
At the unbreakable ground:
Look with your battered mind's
Too consequential sadness.
Do not miss
Those reds, russets, profound dark yellows:
Late, late,
But hardy,
Perennial.

COLLOQUIES

My friend, and what a word that is, in his trouble
Was abandoned, yet he admired her courage
And loved her more for what she had to do,
So that at night when he was reading
He found that her hands, red with his blood,
Were turning the pages; that she'd been standing
On the other sides of walls just before
He opened doors to meet with vacancy.
His books vanished, re-arranged themselves,
And one day his teaspoons
Marched away out into the street
Then back through the hall
And onto the draining board.
He did not wonder at all at this:
Being left had turned his world into magic.

I spoke to her,
For she was my daughter,
Could tell her only 'Anderson wrote:
"Dreiser, the heavy-footed, had tramped
Through the real wilderness of puritan lies,
Making a pathway for us all." '
From his cold house he told me about his troubles
In long telephone calls, and I just listened.

Now I'm in my trouble, of a different kind,
Not abandoned, but bewildered, guilty;
And my world too is full of harrowed magic.
He doesn't even know who she is. Or does he,
And is all impossible love and yearning,
Not like anything else ever, or ever describable?
Not long ago I'd forgotten. But now I ask:
You, who are still young, tell me,
Is it a thing better to talk of only,
Never to try to enact?
What shall I do?
Am I fortunate only to be sick with
The healing disease of her rejection,
Or should I try to cure it?

THE WORD MACHINE

I was so sick with love, and with the hopelessness,
I wandered into wet fields, lay down, and waited to die,
Trying like a sullen child to make her agonize so
                                        that she would
Forever cherish in forlorn tear-stained ribbon
The-more-meaningful-than-ever-she-could-have-believed
Relics of my devotedness.

I lay in a soft sheath of rain muted by half-silence
Whose strange hiss (not the rain's) appalled my
                                        foolish waiting
And the ending of that day.

I found myself searching in the darkness and I half-lived:
I combed the grass towards that hiss for might not it be
The word-machine?
I could smash that with its love love love: that
                                        would be a blow
Identic to the discovery of some herb which purged
The heart of its desire: an act of God which would
                                        transform
A beloved once beautiful into a ravening beast
To flee from in pure terror.

I found only word-eggs, like demons' eyes: scattered
                                        needles
With pulp bursting and burgeoning twistedly
                                through their wood.
My pockets bulged; the newborn wordworms, growing
                                        rapidly,
Writhed. I'd taken them to burn, each and all, but
                                rushed home and fell
Into sleep and into dreams of my successful suicide
And of a ravaged face.

Now they have turned into dawn-diamonds.
Each knifes my waking heart with hope.

NOTHING

Between us there was *nothing*, not a
Look or touch; nor would I fantasize
What had not been; but why do I
About you dream such exact lies
That waking catches me by the throat
With ignoble alchemy? I thought of
Jardins sous la pluie, but we never
In any garden watched rain on flowers.
Nor do you listen to such music.
But your presence so permeates my air
That I immodestly swear
You never quite meant *nothing*,
For *nothing* is some thing:
Is it that single degree you remarked
Makes the difference between snow and rain?
It snowed. But *Jardins sous la pluie*:
Is that now *nothing* even if you never hear it?
No, I cannot accept *nothing*.
Even today it's likely that once
You'll think idly of me – it would be natural –
Then say, oh, *nothing*, to yourself.
And your face thoughtful for the instant
As that *nothing* passes means more to me
Than it could to you. But why should you speak
Of any such *nothings* ever to me?

DIFFERENT IMAGINATIONS

Why must it be that my tenderness for you,
Decently inexplicable in your eyes
Which grow less wounded when I'm with you,
And in your beauty as unobtrusively it grows –
Why must that turn so easily to different
Imaginations which grope as if searching for
Further revelations? I told you that now
I had your trust, and you kissed my lips
As naturally...
              Is that not new
Knowledge enough? Indeed, I'm torn between
The ever-so-fragile thing which is your gift
And grossness which swells, and wanes: how can I know
Unless by wondering half-horribly
But half-devotedly: are you, too, frail?
And what could I return to you in bed
That truly was a greater tenderness?

Damn love for being like history's always made
It seem!
        So this I ask of you, at least:
If it is no more than lust, then despite lust
Don't back away from me again: for you I'm gentle.
Suppose I made you feel loved for long hours
What would you do when I had to go away?
Best then to let me love, do as you wish.
Allow me to have the sadness if I must:
And if desire denied is stronger
Make my tenderness for you last longer!

THE MESSENGER

'It is no longer a Paradise of snakes.
We have brought mankind into it.'
Mrs Gould, passing on, had the
vividness of a figure seen in the
clear patches of sun that chequer the
gloom of open glades in woods.
Conrad, *Nostromo.*

She was so terrified of tenderness
She could not grant a single chance to feel
The rapture of that many-coloured beast,
The messenger who comes for us
From the ancient Paradise of snakes.
She perished day by day, all hope refused.
Because she feared the unknown was a lure.
Although she pursued danger heartlessly,
She would not know it's through itself it fades,
That it's the unmasked face which Nature matches.

She, passing on, had not the vividness
Of figures seen in the bright patches
Of sunlight as it pierces the stern gloom
Of those almost always darkened glades
Which roam the forest wilderness that she and I,
And all of us, must in how much solitude endure?

IN MY EYE

My burned stabbed single seeing eye's a cave agape
On mid-heights unscanned except perhaps
By some mad sheriff with his telescopic
Yearning to pick a rapist off. It watches you,
Empty but for some crumbling bones,
A hundred-thousand-year-old fire,
And the droppings of rabid bats.
No one civil's entered here.
I am this precipice: my eye's
Alive, though cannot glint to draw a shot
From any madman down below – and must endure
Sightless aeons of everlastingness
Like it was blind (think of the past
That's locked in me!). The lid's burned off,
Nor can tears flow: even you at times
I see through the streams that pour
Off my glacial jutting brow
Yards from my gnawed vacancy.
But there are gaps in dry eternity.
When painfully I must unlearn
The secrets of the wreckage which I hold,
As when my gaze was captured by the colours
Of your bright speculations.

And you? You hardly know I watch,
Though this desolateness is yours, not mine:
I'm just the passive part of it.
You are absolute mistress,
If you could bear to take command,
Of disconsolation and the unexplored,
And of whatever lies beyond.
Thousands of miles away I see you,
Knowing you can't avoid your fate,
Handing drinks around, and laughing;
But also I see you in your sleep,
Reading your dreams from the smoke-puffs
Of the madman's rifle down below –

How could he know his frenzy's randomness
Made such a subtle pattern of your woe? —
And I watch when you're alone in sadness
And hopeful numinous imaginings.
Be aware of my charred eye, though not of me,
And of the bloody lichen running down my cheeks;
But let your dreams
And your imaginings look up still higher:
Climb this annihilated steepness
To the mottled menace of the sky above
Which can clear only in an unanguished love.

RACHMANINOV

Rachmaninov put his hands terribly to his head
As he found his own First Symphony
Insupportable
And at the end of the first movement
Fled,
Spent the night on a tramcar
Shuttling backwards and forwards.
It was so garish
That his mind broke down.
But it is well known
How he was hypnotised
And returned in triumph
To compose the Second Concerto.

Now I'm Rachmaninov:
Have seen all that dazzle-in-the-dark
And dark-in-the-dazzle,
Have shuttled with wrecked mind between termini,
Recovered in the sternness
Of an obdurate Russian gaze,
Rediscovered winning musical ways.

Shrunk in my furs I menace
With whistling digits
Auditoria rapturously silent
In the spirit of polite adulterous tearooms.

How do you discern my true melody?
Leave the man you were going to be guilty with,
Come to my dressing-room instead.
Though I'm a melancholy exile
I'll more than tell you what I'm like in bed.
We'll play The Isle of the Dead
And while you go on repeating the perfect truth
That my Preludes are underrated
I'll put my hands terribly to my head.

SILVERHILL

White chairs in a tall stack against a table
In the tiny garden of a pub
On a hill in sleazy St. Leonards;
Greybrick houses cluster all around.
A good district to disappear into.
I watch the chairs through the window.
Are those raindrops? It's overcast,
And so am I. But nothing matches
So well my sorrow as this scene:
Last night, sunny, people had games there,
In that garden. I dwell on their small past
More keenly than they. I have a pang
At my heart, but know it's my own mind
Hurting it – that it's no longer you.
I must have wanted you to be unkind.

Walking now, I pass an entrance flanked
By two open-beaked stone birds-of-prey.
The whitewash hardly covering their grey.
A child has stuck into each mouth
A carnation ripped off just as it bloomed.
Each bird stares greyly at me from beneath
Its flakily whitened eye.
More befalls than thought, speech, action,
In the ominous air,
Like that table, that clambering top chair
Crookedly stuck into the darkening sky.

You spread that menace, but cannot care:
Play no part in this presageful fable
From which I flee – but to whom, and where?

APRES UN REVE

It was as if I were widely awake
When you, half-Madonna
With child as if torn from your embrace
Said hushed and alone from a moonlit niche
'Come with me for your mind-fuck.'
We walked together upwards
Towards an unknown sky
Neither wanting from the other
More than warmth and sympathy.
Despite the moon I should have known
Better than to trust such luck –
I, who had never, in love, said fuck.

Now it is customary day
And you are cold and shy away
From my smallest glance
And when I ask why it cannot be
In undream as in dream you say
'I don't like luck'
And are sullenly reticent.

You know you were in that dream
But did you put yourself there,
And did you say what I heard you say?

The owl awakes from her day-long sleep
And I await the dark
Though knowing that, perplexed,
I may not find sleep.
I am thus exposed, whatever I do,
To night's inviolable deceit –
If not to a dream that is a cheat
Then to a moonlessness which hides
Your knowledge of me, your true needs,
As with closed eyes you beside me lie –

135

BEING INVENTED YOU

Being invented you to test itself
And that all things went cross-grained with me
Because of it, was no issue in
Such engines (are they?) as make creatures
Of desire like you. Endearments you
Forbade, and, as well, mute attendance;
It made my ferocious rococo
Strict, as not before. Forgive me though
If in uneasy sleep I mutter
Your name; not even I shall know it;
Nor are you in my dreams what you were
In others': unvictim now, and free.

POOL OF LIGHT

The air is bewitched around my red lamp's
Pool of light
When on the wire your voice
Charged with your whole body's warmth
Whispers good night good night.

THE LOVE TOUCAN

You told me I was like some bird
As if I could fly willingly away
To some forest not near you.
But there I'd be unfree:
Know your enchantingness,
Don't let me drain your eyes
Of their new green,
Let me be by you in a cage
All night, all day,
And, though I cannot sing,
Love you with my hoarse cries.

136

THE SHAWL

Dawn's icy snarl of circumstance
Obtrudes, yet cannot obtrude
Into our companionship
Of the night before:
Enraptured by some shore
Which we have never seen
But imagine may have been.
What can we do but celebrate
Our togethered differentness
Though there — but not yet there?

Suddenly I saw this morning
Through your doom-packed face
Clear eyes, green and sparkling,
Of which you did not know —
Though, checked by my own defeat,
I could not tell you of them.

But through that day I stayed
(As you remember well)
And now tonight I do, and now circumstance's
No more than your old shawl
Which you spread across our knees, to share
Against a more familiar chill.
And aren't we companions still?

YOUR LOOK

Sweetheart, when I praise the lucid look
You give me, I don't delude myself
That you're without perfidy, or that you're perfect.
Who does not, looking at another, wonder
Though without narrowing the eyes in hurtful appraisal,
'Is he the one I want? Do I want anyone?'
Or ponder
'Is he more treacherous than he acts
And could he help it if he were
More than any other love?'
'Why do I feel half-trapped here?
Where's my freedom and what
Is my freedom?'

No, I mean only this:
That green discovers its nature in your gaze –
Green, which is ambiguous although
It gives beauty to what life there is.
Dear one, that's just the way things are:
There's honour, as well as blame
In the tree and where it stands.

So after all it's simple:
Just the whole world's green
Is what I praise.
What better, in loving you,
Despite the way things are,
Could I do?
Green, in your candour, finds itself
Calculation falls away, and you are you.
So all those perfidies are safe
Because you trust me
With such an artless, and benevolent, anxiety.

APPETITE OF QUIET ENCHANTMENT

An abandoned mandolin
Lies, still unrotted, on a stone in the jungle
Where you have been, and I have not.
The wind stirs faintly its strings.

Here it is chill, the leaves scrape the ground already,
There is no mandolin,
There is sadness here because there is no mandolin,
No jungle where you have been and I have not,
Nor record of the ignorant wanderer
Who left it where he did.
But a sort of music, from my garden
Stirs faintly my stretched nerves,
My nerves which ought not to be stretched.
I cannot understand it, but,
Although my curiosity's so great,
I will not question it.
In my dreams of that mandolin
I am asking a question;
I fear the sound the wind makes in it,
I fear to understand it,
I fear to sleep, and in waking even,
Afraid, avoid all reverie.
I do not want to know why I left that mandolin
In the jungle where you have been and I have not.
I am afraid of your world.
I love you. But how can I love you perfectly?
Your knowingness is of the mandolin
And of why I left it
In the jungle where you have been and I have not.

MARS IN SCORPIO

I am full of fate, drifting in an oarless boat
Through dank boundless water towards the final ice.
From whence the yellow leaves floating?
Do you, a wind stripping trees far away there,
Send them in a hapless sympathy which you deny,
Or are they emblems of my destructiveness
(The fire and ardency of that seem now so far away)?
Whichever, since I'm in such solitude,
You can for me be nothing other than the sullen sky,
The sullen sky above and in these
Dead waters in which its reflection's broken by
The dismal leaves which skimming here
Show both your long desire
For me, and its decay;
You can for me be nothing other than the sullen sky
And my approaching night.
I am my fate at last: almost becalmed, but
Heading, on this stern lacustrine mirror of your justice
Towards such intensities of cold that I've no choice
But between fear, and fear.
How more and yet more frozenly must I aspire
To be consumed in the flames of our old fire?

THERE WAS NEVER

There was never silence so eloquent
Amongst stars quivering in pure air above cloud.
It can wander where it wants to wander,
The by-fate-defeated,
As along this path, this as-the-crow-flies distance
With which love punishes the miles between us.

Kneeling in the room's centre I saw above me,
In the pane suspended, a cold new moon.
I wanted to go into the air to view it
Not through glass, to salute your refusal of loss.
But it was too cold for me.

And so I acted out once again
The betrayal of you which you refuse
So lethal and so soon –

And again you say you share it,
This cowardice beneath the moon,
So lethal and so soon.

FORGIVE US, WOMEN

Forgive us, women, that we descend:
High altitudes can cause such anguish.
And forgive us if, when we come down,
We drive off, jaws clenched, across the plain
Fleeing the looming shadow of the range.
The towns and villages pass us by
On the road's dead ribbon – swoosh, swoosh, swoosh –
In daze; we can't stop to speak one word,
Don't ever want the tragic journey
To come to an end, we're so alone.
Why can't we say we need your sorrow,
Or think of you, up there on the heights,
Who know our pain matches your pain,
And how they're matchless as the flatlands
Look, a lucid green, but stormy-edged?
Our only certainty's to drive on,
Awaiting the sea which will halt us.
But worst of all's this hard pitiless
Ungentle, cruel, incessant rain.

AFTER TAGORE

We know the time has come for me to go,
Leave you alone. I now will be your weather
Chiding you with violent rain and storm
And caressing you with gentle breezes –
We still live under the same sun –
And I will be as much no part of you
As weather's not when you're in bed,
And I will be as much a part of you
As weather has to be when you go out.

A SORT OF LOVE

Friendship's so difficult, for being a sort of love
It makes confusions about love, and undermines
The candour of exchanging that it has to be.
A sunshaft, sudden, wintry-low, reveals the dust
In the heart's room: takes us unawares,
And frightens us with unfamiliarity.
We watch it settle, but are too mesmerised,
And then a cloud obscures the sun too soon –
We wait for darkness but forget its dangers:
How could we watch dust in even the luckiest moon?
Thus in my confusion, aching to give, I gave you pain,
And just as you have to go away, to Vienna – all faith
In me destroyed. What can I tell you, ask you,
To restore your trust?
                    Walk in the Prater, alone –
For yourself, not me – where Wittgenstein ogled
The mindless youths: *Die Welt ist alles, was der Fall ist.*
Let it be the case that wandering flakes of snow,
Crystals as innocent and delicate as you,
Fall on your shoulders – though not to chill you more –
And fall too on the empty park's expanse.
Feel the wisdom of the scene (but for yourself,
Not me). Although I'm helpless in my sin
Against one so gentle, as I am against nature's fitfulness
(The sun may shine brightly in a clear blue sky!)
I still urge the weather there to do this for you
In hope you'll understand how friendship wants to be:
Weightless upon you, silent, loving the way you see
Small solitary truths, and so once more might discover it
(For yourself) somehow in even me.

THE INTERNAL SABOTEUR

I twitch and jerk on my nerves' piano-wire
A traitor to a cursed cause self-condemned,
Nor can the obscene execution end.
Look at the evidences of desire:
At how I die, and die, bizarre metaphor
For my loveless effort to live more and more
And yet defeat my concupiscent part!

Corrupted conscience, could it be but heart:
Allow an unpled innocence to start.
But black duty's the internal saboteur
Determines the penalties I must incur –
Trapped in the passion of fanatic thought
I presided over that infamous court
And as I dance upon the cutting ligature
Watch myself on film, as ordered, to make sure
That I squirm justly in the eternal pure.

If I could only hear the animal speak
I should be spared such trials, and such defeat;
I could transform that stuprate saboteur
Into a friend who'd bind us all together
And make my heart into the thinking part.

My heart's a beast whose words come from my head
But as here I jounce, nothing can be said
Until this internal saboteur is dead:
Give me the grace at last to understand
The language of God's creatures at their end.
There's such divinity within their lack
As would give me my conversation back.

REFLECTIONS

For you the mirror's water,
Your world its: silent and still
Or shallow and flowing fast, or deep
And idling by, swaying the lilies
Of your imagination as easily
As you don't know your mercy.
Without exercitation you set right
Your face, seek neither good nor ill,
So mindful are you, dearest heart,
Of what sort of weather reigns
In that paradise of yours
Where fanged animals bask
Unthreatening in the sun.
While the gentle may kill...

Don't wonder if I'm desolate
That in bleaknesses you need
To be told you're beautiful:
That even your deep sparkling gaze
Can be disenchanted by
Dirty rains from a wrong sky.

For me the mirror was silver,
Its lie meticulous.
Each day I mirror-wrote myself
And lived on its wrong side –
To suit each day's need
And each day's wrong desire –
I never know how I lied
Until I met you here
As real in your dismay
As you are anywhere.

So now I hold up these words
To a different kind of glass:
Shattered to a million cracks

By the explosion of a will
That even unhappy's beautiful.
Dulled in its frame it has not got
One single smooth bright spot
And you look out at me from there
Whether you care or do not care
So desperate and clear
I know it's not that man me
You seem to watch so carefully
From that opaque and self-denying sea.

EYEBRIGHT

Desolate, searching for you, this evening –
All traffic-sounds and children's cries,
Even the song of birds,
Extraneous, I image you, and thus coldly learn
You're really not by my side. But your eyes,
Though clouded with pain, are in that image bright.
Beloved, menacing, but never fatal gift,
Your enchantment of me cannot but be perilous.
Knowing you not blessed enough I seek
To cast upon you some of your own light
And yet for myself, somehow, seem not to speak.
So deny me. Be my flower not striving to make
Any love but for your own sweet sake.

LETTERS

A bloody rorschach
Stains the chlorotic sky
Of this ash-written day.
Transforms my letters to you
Into a cinereous alphabet.

I do not want to challenge you
Or be an I who, since its futurity
Invaded your gaze, must stand and suffer
Hundredly your infallible destiny,
Face writhing like a mirror of your pain.

My days are disabled
By my history:
How could I say
'You are my Alpha'
Without your eyes clouding over
With multifarious qualms,
Closing to shut off with smooth lids
That half-doubtful, half-enchanted look?
How much is it my unripeness
That you're not resistible
In this land of chattering dead?

Your moon in ice and my moon in water
Are the same moon. I tremble
As I remember
When I was not there:
Your grief as you watched alone
Your heart's moon broken
In the spume of waterfalls.

Don't let this chlorotic sky, or my letters,
Make you weep.
Be in your old heart entire, asleep —

Watched over not by me
But by my desire to keep
You enclosed forever
In ancient undefeat.

Don't weep because I weep.

SHE TO HIM

Question: Do You Reprove Me for Loving You?

No, I don't reprove. But I must condemn
Your lie. You see, although I am myself
Warm, human and without pretence,
Ready to come to your defence,
Also I'm what you make me, Queen of Darkness,
And so must see you damned. Perhaps otherwise
I'd hold you in my arms and kiss and comfort you:
Ah, luxuriate in what that bliss could be
If you would only unimagine me!

TO MY DAUGHTERS

My child (whichever) my love for you's more dear
As fatherhood becomes more clear.
Now I can no longer bear
Not to be my own ghost spying
On your mind after my dying:
Sitting in a shaft of this same sun,
Going through my dusty stuff and saying:
'This was his but does not matter any more
Nor did it ever much. Moon in Cancer,
Always he felt compelled
Crab-like to collect
Detritus of a past which now's
No longer anyone's at all,
Unless the Moon's.'

But what is never past, my child (whichever)
Is my blessing on you
As adamantine now as when I saw you first.
Love like mine for you's almost
To much to bear
And undoes history quite.
It never can be told except
Beyond death's care, as now;
But then it's as heartfelt as the sun is warm.
Now, as you muse upon these relics,
Now, as I write you these words.

Index of first lines

A bloody rorschach   147
A fortunemaster, whom the sun selected   23
A week-end at last in his splendid castle,   8
All her devils here tonight,   33
An abandoned mandolin   139
An ill wind blowing, the fearful man   25
At my utmost North of endeavour,   44

Beach, poetical Wrexham wine-merchant,   110
Being invented you to test itself   136
Bells for a death rang early   28
Between us, the summer evening,   119
Between us there was *nothing*, not a   128
Bring Norma   87

Come with me to Heligoland. It's now   85
Crowding her hours   14

Dangerous in my Y-fronts   78
Dank. Our shared world shattered, ended.   122
Dawn's icy snarl of circumstance   137
'Dear One: 59
Desolate, searching for you, this evening –   146
Do I cause you to do this? Or is it   103
Dreamer, there are no synonyms   32

Early fell to the spell of   95
Everybody's chrysanthemums,   125

For the master who is limiting freedom   65
For you the mirror's water,   145
Forgive us, women, that we descend: 142
Friendship's so difficult, for being a sort of love   143

Goodbye common history   89

Half-heartedly at noon in the market-place,   97

Handsomest of all men now beyond the range,   18
Have you been the victim of a mistake?   108
He came to visit me, my mortal messenger;   3
He sought to define the shape of her love: 27
Helljoy. When I remark or leer, your eyes   107
Her other lover in a hated city   7
Her violent birds in his head he wished   33
How few are not possessed by private joy   41
How will you destroy me, love?   26

I am full of fate, drifting in an oarless boat   140
I climbed to the Fifth up the dangerous tube   113
I found her hovering, beautiful   9
I held you close O warm you lay   43
I know that before a storm my hands   5
I left you Norma and you died alone   90
I met you, Norma, dearly young,   86
I see you are puzzled in your endless queues   49
I sit wanting   109
I smooth out a map of where I live,   82
I twitch and jerk on my nerves' piano-wire   144
I used to be a stanzaic boy, conned the porters
        at Christchurch,   76
I was a young man once   121
I was asked to compile a Dictionary   96
I was so sick with love, and with the hopelessness,   127
I woke on top of a lichenous mountain   50
In his rare spasms does censor Jack shout out   73
In that cloud of grief at our private farewell   13
In the administration of culture,   60
It is well for you tonight pretty girl   82
It was a stranger child, she knows, than I   31
It was as if I were widely awake   135
I've had too much trouble in my life.   104

Just when I was still contented   80

Lancelot's last and only love was merely   17
La Pasionaria, what's permitted?   70

152

Love is a dead image, treeless pool changing   35
Mr Tropayoz,   105
My burned stabbed single seeing eye's a cave agape   131
My child (whichever) my love for you's more dear   149
My friend, and what a word that is, in his trouble   126
My mind created you as I emerged   118

Nature has left too many relics here.   62
No one will know these houses are the same   34
No vows these days   90

O harlequin, you know too late   16
Of all men living who could be most wise   40
'One of the best of a valuable series...'   88

Pasty, with brazen curls, you dream away   84
Pinchbeck, constructor of automata and other desiderata,   98
Podge (the unloved one in you, even,   64
Poets pretend   81
Privately to you and while confined   94

Question: Do You Reprove Me for Loving You?   148

Rachmaninov put his hands terribly to his head   133
Reaching hear watch wind   120

Sado-pathic, thanks for drawing   73
Secret dwarf pornographers who live   77
She is afraid of dawn, a sin in hope   15
She was so terrified of tenderness   130
She went out, for a moment, she said –   92
She wounded him and bound his wound,   3
Somewhere great life streams choicelessly   114
Stand on this shore and watch – the sea   19
Sweetheart, remember those small hours when time's   117
Sweetheart, when I praise the lucid look   138

That hag with you there   106
The air is bewitched round my red lamp's   136
The bells ring signal of judgement at last,   39
The big day dawned. They had not told me.   57

The drowned know the sea is wounded   39
The mind destroys the scene before it sees: 46
The monuments had gone.   100
The new girl with violent hair   83
The preliminaries to your death are   99
The prime minister (the man himself, of course)   54
Then turn your head. It is easy   16
There are some no times   119
There was never silence so eloquent   141
They were servants of a beauty   32
This green wall to which I turn for sleep   4
This little love-God is a shit, brown-suited,   91
This morning over the town   6
This side of love, the island is   10
Thomas the Wastrel, the Pay-Corps Colonel,   66
Those eyes of mine in nineteen-ten   79
Through disaster I turn poet monthly   111
Toupée askew after the dusty journey   71
Trapped as the Church disgorges   74

Upon men of unfortunately strong emotións,   75

Walked in the rain to post you a letter.   124
Watch what the sun can do, because you died   26
We know the time has come for me to go,   142
What schoolmasters say is not always wrong,   42
When I was broken down and unemployed   63
White chairs in a tall stack against a table   134
Why live at all? Absurd question.   95
Why must it be that my tenderness for you,   129
Winter for William, who lives far off   12

Yesterday I took you to a place   86
You asked me, 'do you still love me?'   123
You told me I was like some bird   136

Index of Titles

Administrators, The 60
After Tagore 142
All Devils Fading 33
Answer, The 95
Appetite of Quiet Enchantment 139
Après un Rêve 135

Beach, 1737 110
Beauty and the Beast 19
Being Invented You 136
Birds in his Head 33
Blitzenkrieger 50
Blue Trumpeter, The 94

Cellar, The 100
Censor Jack 73
Change, The 43
Child after a Storm 5
Chrysanthemums 125
Colloquies 126
Cruel Gravy, The 76
Cursed Harlequin 16

Dead Lover, The 28
Despair 9
Different Imaginations 129
Don Juan in Hell 18

Elegy 31
Entrance to Hell 13
Execution, The 57
Eyebright 146

Federico Garcia Lorca: 1910 (Interval) 79
Fernando Pessoa: Poets 81
Flight of a Dove 6

Forgive Us, Women   142
Forthcoming Attractions   41
Fortunemaster   23
Found on a Building Site   59
Furies   32

Girl's Song   105
Green Wall My Grave   4

He Came to Visit Me   3
History Lesson   65

I Have Never Felt   75
I Was a Young Man Once   121
Imagined Child   7
In Memoriam Brian Higgins 1930-1965   109
In My Eye   131
In the Hotel   113
In the Market-Place   97
Infant Man, The   25
Influenzal   120
Internal Saboteur, The   144
Invitation, The   71

Lancelot   17
Last Chance, The   54
Letters   147
Lights on the Water, The   39
Living by the River   62
Lonely Ghost, The   118
Love Toucan, The   136

Mars in Scorpio   140
Men of the Island   10
Messenger, The   130
Mistral   92
Mother in Sunlight, A   14

New Year   16
No One Will Know   34

North   119
Northern Monster, The   44
Nothing   128

Observation for Unverifiable Reconsideration
    in a Game Perhaps, An   99
Obstacles   119

Pathétique   95
Pinchbeck   98
Pool, The   35
Pool of Light   136
Poor Fatso   64
Punishment, The   40

Queen Leer   73
Questions before Parting   108
Questions on the Staircase   26

Rachmaninov   133
Reflections   145
Reminiscences of Norma   82
Request on the Field   63
Rosy Captain, The   46

Sacrifice, The   3
Saxelby   96
Scrap of Moonlight, A   124
Shape of Love, The   27
Shawl, The   137
She Is Afraid of Dawn   15
She to Him   148
Shore, The   114
Silverhill   134
Sort of Love, A   143
Speech from a Play   107
Sunday Morning Walk   74

Tea with Miss Stockport   66
There was Never   141
To All Watchers over Public Morality   77

To Miss Parfitt (1934) Sadly: This Poem about Dying   104
To My Daughters   149
To My Wife in Hospital   123
To Passers-By   49
To Sally Chilver   70
Trial in Dream, A   32
Tuthill's Enormities   111

Umberto Saba: Winter Noon   80
Unsmiling   122
Versifier in Private, A   78
Victims, The   39
Voyage to an Island   20

Week-End   8
What Schoolmasters Say   42
Why   103
Wilderness   117
Winter for William   12
Word Machine, The   127
Words, The   107

Your Look   138

GREENWICH EXCHANGE BOOKS

All books are paperbacks unless otherwise stated

POETRY

Adam's Thoughts in Winter *by Warren Hope*
Warren Hope's poems have appeared from time to time in a number of literary periodicals, pamphlets and anthologies on both sides of the Atlantic. They appeal to lovers of poetry everywhere. His poems are brief, clear, frequently lyrical, characterised by wit, but often distinguished by tenderness. The poems gathered in this first book-length collection counter the brutalising ethos of contemporary life, speaking of and for the virtues of modesty, honesty and gentleness in an individual, memorable way.
Warren Hope is a poet, a critic and university lecturer. He lives and works in Philadelphia, where he raised his family.
2000 • 54 pages • ISBN 1-871551-40-4

Baudelaire: Les Fleurs du Mal *Translated by F.W. Leakey*
Selected poems from *Les Fleurs du Mal* are translated with parallel French texts and are designed to be read with pleasure by readers who have no French as well as those who are practised in the French language.
F.W. Leakey was Professor of French in the University of London. As a scholar, critic and teacher he specialised in the work of Baudelaire for 50 years and published a number of books on the poet.
2001 • 152 pages • ISBN 1-871551-10-2

'The Last Blackbird' and other poems by Ralph Hodgson *edited and introduced by John Harding*
Ralph Hodgson (1871-1962) was a poet and illustrator whose most influential and enduring work appeared to great acclaim just prior to and during the First World War. His work is imbued with a spiritual passion for the beauty of creation and the mystery of existence. This new selection brings together, for the first time in 40 years, some of the most beautiful and powerful 'hymns to life' in the English language.
John Harding lives in London. He is a freelance writer and teacher and is Ralph Hodgson's biographer.
2004 • 64 pages • ISBN 1-871551-81-1

Lines from the Stone Age *by Sean Haldane*
Reviewing Sean Haldane's 1992 volume *Desire in Belfast*, Robert Nye wrote in *The Times* that "Haldane can be sure of his place among the English

poets." This place is not yet a conspicuous one, mainly because his early volumes appeared in Canada and because he has earned his living by other means than literature. Despite this, his poems have always had their circle of readers. The 60 previously unpublished poems of *Lines from the Stone Age* – "lines of longing, terror, pride, lust and pain" – may widen this circle.
2000 • 52 pages • ISBN 1-871551-39-0

The Rain and the Glass – 99 Poems, New and Selected *by Robert Nye*
This book contains all the poems Nye has written since his *Collected Poems* of 1995, together with his own selection from that volume. An introduction, telling the story of his poetic beginnings, affirms Nye's unfashionable belief in inspiration, as well as defining that quality of unforced truth which distinguishes the best of his work: "I have spent my life trying to write poems, but the poems gathered here came mostly when I was not."
2004 • 132 pages • ISBN 1-871551-41-2

Shakespeare's Sonnets *by Martin Seymour-Smith*
Martin Seymour-Smith's outstanding achievement lies in the field of literary biography and criticism. In 1963 he produced his comprehensive edition, in the old spelling, of *Shakespeare's Sonnets* (here revised and corrected by himself and Peter Davies in 1998). With its landmark introduction and its brilliant critical commentary on each sonnet, it was praised by William Empson and John Dover Wilson. Stephen Spender said of him "I greatly admire Martin Seymour-Smith for the independence of his views and the great interest of his mind"; and both Robert Graves and Anthony Burgess described him as the leading critic of his time. His exegesis of the *Sonnets* remains unsurpassed.
2001 • 194 pages • ISBN 1-871551-38-2

Wilderness *by Martin Seymour-Smith*
This is Martin Seymour-Smith's first publication of his poetry for more than twenty years. This collection of 36 poems is a fearless account of an inner life of love, frustration, guilt, laughter and the celebration of others. He is best known to the general public as the author of the controversial and bestselling *Hardy* (1994).
1994 • 52 pages • ISBN 1-871551-08-0

LITERATURE & BIOGRAPHY

Matthew Arnold and 'Thyrsis' *by Patrick Carill Connolly*
Matthew Arnold (1822-1888) was a leading poet, intellect and aesthete of
the Victorian epoch. He is now best known for his strictures as a literary
and cultural critic, and educationist. After a long period of neglect, his
views have come in for a re-evaluation. Arnold's poetry remains less well
known, yet his poems and his understanding of poetry, which defied the
conventions of his time, were central to his achievement.
The author traces Arnold's intellectual and poetic development, showing
how his poetry gathers its meanings from a lifetime's study of European
literature and philosophy. Connolly's unique exegesis of 'Thyrsis' draws
upon a wide-ranging analysis of the pastoral and its associated myths in
both classical and native cultures. This study shows lucidly and in detail
how Arnold encouraged the intense reflection of the mind on the subject
placed before it, believing in " … the all importance of the choice of the
subject, the necessity of accurate observation; and subordinate character
of expression."
Patrick Carill Connolly gained his English degree at Reading University
and taught English literature abroad for a number of years before returning
to Britain. He is now a civil servant living in London.
2004 • 180 pages • ISBN 1-871551-61-7

The Author, the Book and the Reader *by Robert Giddings*
This collection of essays analyses the effects of changing technology and
the attendant commercial pressures on literary styles and subject matter.
Authors covered include Charles Dickens, Tobias Smollett, Mark Twain,
Dr Johnson and John le Carré.
Robert Giddings, formerly Professor in the School of Media, Arts and
Communications at Bournemouth University, is a well-established literary
critic and cultural historian.
1991 • 220 pages • illustrated • ISBN 1-871551-01-3

Aleister Crowley and the Cult of Pan *by Paul Newman*
Few more nightmarish figures stalk English literature than Aleister Crowley
(1875-1947), poet, magician, mountaineer and agent provocateur. In this
groundbreaking study, Paul Newman dives into the occult mire of Crowley's
works and fishes out gems and grotesqueries that are by turns ethereal,
sublime, pornographic and horrifying. Like Oscar Wilde before him,
Crowley stood in "symbolic relationship to his age" and to contemporaries
like Rupert Brooke, G.K. Chesterton and the Portuguese modernist,
Fernando Pessoa. An influential exponent of the cult of the Great God Pan,

his essentially 'pagan' outlook was shared by major European writers as well as English novelists like E.M. Forster, D.H. Lawrence and Arthur Machen.

Paul Newman lives in Cornwall. Editor of the literary magazine *Abraxas*, he has written more than ten books.

2004 • 222 pages • ISBN 1-871551-66-8

John Dryden *by Anthony Fowles*
Of all the poets of the Augustan age, John Dryden was the most worldly. Anthony Fowles traces Dryden's evolution from 'wordsmith' to major poet. This critical study shows a poet of vigour and technical panache whose art was forged in the heat and battle of a turbulent polemical and pamphleteering age. Although Dryden's status as a literary critic has long been established, Fowles draws attention to his neglected achievements as a translator of poetry. He deals also with the less well-known aspects of Dryden's work – his plays and occasional pieces.

Born in London and educated at the Universities of Oxford and Southern California, Anthony Fowles began his career in filmmaking before becoming an author of film and television scripts and more than twenty books. Readers will welcome the many contemporary references to novels and film with which Fowles illuminates the life and work of this decisively influential English poetic voice.

2003 • 292 pages • ISBN 1-871551-58-7

The Good That We Do *by John Lucas*
John Lucas' book blends fiction, biography and social history in order to tell the story of his grandfather, Horace Kelly. Headteacher of a succession of elementary schools in impoverished areas of London, 'Hod' Kelly was also a keen cricketer, a devotee of the music hall, and included among his friends the great trade union leader, Ernest Bevin. In telling the story of his life, Lucas has provided a fascinating range of insights into the lives of ordinary Londoners from the First World War until the outbreak of the Second World War. Threaded throughout is an account of such people's hunger for education, and of the different ways government, church and educational officialdom ministered to that hunger. *The Good That We Do* is both a study of one man and of a period when England changed, drastically and forever.

John Lucas is Professor Emeritus of English at the Universities of Loughborough and Nottingham Trent.

2001 • 214 pages • ISBN 1-871551-54-4

In Pursuit of Lewis Carroll *by Raphael Shaberman*
Sherlock Holmes and the author uncover new evidence in their investigations into the mysterious life and writing of Lewis Carroll. They examine published works by Carroll that have been overlooked by previous commentators. A newly discovered poem, almost certainly by Carroll, is published here.

Amongst many aspects of Carroll's highly complex personality, this book explores his relationship with his parents, numerous child friends, and the formidable Mrs Liddell, mother of the immortal Alice.

Raphael Shaberman was a founder member of the Lewis Carroll Society and a teacher of autistic children.

1994 • 118 pages • illustrated • ISBN 1-871551-13-7

Liar! Liar!: Jack Kerouac – Novelist *by R.J. Ellis*
The fullest study of Jack Kerouac's fiction to date. It is the first book to devote an individual chapter to every one of his novels. *On the Road*, *Visions of Cody* and *The Subterraneans* are reread in-depth, in a new and exciting way. *Visions of Gerard* and *Doctor Sax* are also strikingly reinterpreted, as are other daringly innovative writings, like 'The Railroad Earth' and his "try at a spontaneous *Finnegans Wake*" – *Old Angel Midnight*. Neglected writings, such as *Tristessa* and *Big Sur*, are also analysed, alongside better-known novels such as *Dharma Bums* and *Desolation Angels*.

R.J. Ellis is Senior Lecturer in English at Nottingham Trent University.

1999 • 294 pages • ISBN 1-871551-53-6

Musical Offering *by Yolanthe Leigh*
In a series of vivid sketches, anecdotes and reflections, Yolanthe Leigh tells the story of her growing up in the Poland of the 1930s and the Second World War. These are poignant episodes of a child's first encounters with both the enchantments and the cruelties of the world; and from a later time, stark memories of the brutality of the Nazi invasion, and the hardships of student life in Warsaw under the Occupation. But most of all this is a record of inward development; passages of remarkable intensity and simplicity describe the girl's response to religion, to music, and to her discovery of philosophy.

Yolanthe Leigh was formerly a Lecturer in Philosophy at Reading University.

2000 • 56 pages • ISBN: 1-871551-46-3

Norman Cameron *by Warren Hope*
Norman Cameron's poetry was admired by W.H. Auden, celebrated by Dylan Thomas and valued by Robert Graves. He was described by Martin

Seymour-Smith as, "one of ... the most rewarding and pure poets of his generation ..." and is at last given a full length biography. This eminently sociable man, who had periods of darkness and despair, wrote little poetry by comparison with others of his time, but always of a consistently high quality – imaginative and profound.

2000 • 220 pages • illustrated • ISBN 1-871551-05-6

STUDENT GUIDE LITERARY SERIES

The Greenwich Exchange Student Guide Literary Series is a collection of critical essays of major or contemporary serious writers in English and selected European languages. The series is for the student, the teacher and 'common readers' and is an ideal resource for libraries. The *Times Educational Supplement* praised these books, saying, "The style of [this series] has a pressure of meaning behind it. Readers should learn from that ... If art is about selection, perception and taste, then this is it."

(ISBN prefix 1-871551- applies)
All books are paperbacks unless otherwise stated

The series includes:
W.H. Auden by Stephen Wade (36-6)
Honoré de Balzac by Wendy Mercer (48-X)
William Blake by Peter Davies (27-7)
The Brontës by Peter Davies (24-2)
Robert Browning by John Lucas (59-5)
Byron by Andrew Keanie (83-9)
Samuel Taylor Coleridge by Andrew Keanie (64-1)
Joseph Conrad by Martin Seymour-Smith (18-8)
William Cowper by Michael Thorn (25-0)
Charles Dickens by Robert Giddings (26-9)
Emily Dickinson by Marnie Pomeroy (68-4)
John Donne by Sean Haldane (23-4)
Ford Madox Ford by Anthony Fowles (63-3)
The Stagecraft of Brian Friel by David Grant (74-9)
Robert Frost by Warren Hope (70-6)
Thomas Hardy by Sean Haldane (33-1)
Seamus Heaney by Warren Hope (37-4)
Joseph Heller by Anthony Fowles (84-6)
Gerard Manley Hopkins by Sean Sheehan (77-3)
James Joyce by Michael Murphy (73-0)
Laughter in the Dark – The Plays of Joe Orton by Arthur Burke (56-0)

Philip Larkin by Warren Hope (35-8)
Poets of the First World War by John Greening (79-X)
Philip Roth by Paul McDonald (72-2)
Shakespeare's *Macbeth* by Matt Simpson (69-2)
Shakespeare's *Othello* by Matt Simpson (71-4)
Shakespeare's *The Tempest* by Matt Simpson (75-7)
Shakespeare's *Twelfth Night* by Matt Simpson (86-2)
Shakespeare's Non-Dramatic Poetry by Martin Seymour-Smith (22-6)
Shakespeare's Sonnets by Martin Seymour-Smith (38-2)
Shakespeare's *The Winter's Tale* by John Lucas (80-3)
Tobias Smollett by Robert Giddings (21-8)
Dylan Thomas by Peter Davies (78-1)
Alfred, Lord Tennyson by Michael Thorn (20-X)
William Wordsworth by Andrew Keanie (57-9)
W.B. Yeats by John Greening (34-X)